Readings in
Money and Banking

Edited by

Harold A. Wolf
and
R. Conrad Doenges
Both at University of Texas

Readings in
Money and Banking

New York

Appleton-Century-Crofts
Educational Division
Meredith Corporation

Preface

In recent years courses in money and banking have been widened to include fiscal policy as well as debt management. This is perhaps a reflection of the view that money and banking, monetary theory, monetary policy, fiscal policy, and debt management are all intertwined. The purpose or goal of monetary policy is the same as the purpose of fiscal policy and that of debt management; they are three kits of policy tools that can be used to accomplish the same purpose. The readings in this book have been selected with that understanding in mind.

We speak of stability as the goal. But do we mean stability of price level; employment and output; or both of these? In any case, we do not want merely stability, but rather a high-level or full-employment stability. In recent years economic growth has become another desideratum of stabilization policy. What is desired now is full-employment—price stability with a high rate of economic growth.

Some have suggested that an additional goal of monetary-fiscal policy should be to eliminate the deficit in the balance of payments, or that, at the very least, the balance-of-payments deficit imposes a restraint on policy.

From these areas of concern we have selected readings to supplement the regular materials used in courses in money and banking, monetary policy, and fiscal policy. Also included are a few articles which deal with the institutional framework within which policy must take place. For example, the structure of the commercial banking system has drawn considerable attention recently. At one time, not long ago, this was considered a dead area. It was not considered important whether or not there was "sufficient" competition in banking, because it was a regulated industry. Recently, the regulatory agencies, as well as the banking community, have taken a second look.

Articles in this area and the others mentioned above were selected with the hope that they would give the student an appreciation for the latest thinking in these areas. They include ideas so new or tentative that textbooks cannot treat them fully.

Grateful acknowledgment is given to the publishers and authors for their permission to reprint these articles. In addition, we wish to extend our appreciation to Nettie Webb, Jane King, Mary Rivers, Joan Rider, and Bernice Wilson for their assistance.

H.A.W.
R.C.D.

Contents

I

The Structure and Operations of Commercial Banks

Commercial banks are part of the institutional structure in the United States that creates money. As the economy grows, the nation's money supply must grow with it. The commercial banks, under the supervision of the Federal Reserve System, provide this enlarged money supply. When banks make loans and investments, they create demand deposits which are money. Commercial banks, however, are more passive than active in the process of creating money. That is, they are more like a sponge in releasing and soaking up money in accordance with the needs of business.

Commercial banks are unique among all private financial institutions in being able to create money, and this has been one of the justifications for greater regulatory controls over commercial banks than over other financial institutions. It has also been generally assumed by the regulatory agencies that, because banks are unique and controlled, there should not be excessive competition in banking. We do not have free entry into banking; rather, the would-be banker must show, to the satisfaction of the regulatory agencies, that a new bank would serve the public need. If the regulatory authorities feel a new charter would increase competition too much, it will be denied. Lately, because of the growth of mergers and the acquisition of more banks by holding companies, the question has been raised, is there enough competition in banking? This thorny question is examined in an article by Almarin Phillips.

Paul M. Horvitz in his article also examines competition in banking and suggests that the regulatory agencies themselves could increase competition by certain administrative decisions. Howard D. Crosse in his article indicates that it is the quality of management more than the degree of concentration which determines the degree of competition in banking.

Related to the problem of competition in banking is the relationship of branch banks to unit banks. It has always been assumed that branch banks are more efficient than unit banks. An article by George J. Benston examines this question and comes up with some interesting data.

A second article by Benston examines whether or not banks discriminate against small borrowers. It has generally been assumed that discrimination exists during periods of tight money. The Benston article questions this assumption.

1

Competition, confusion, and commercial banking*

Almarin Phillips†

The recent interest in competition in the commercial banking industry is a strange turn of events. Not long ago it was customary to refer to banking as one of the "regulated" industries—an industry in which competition had to be restricted by public authority to preserve the liquidity of the payments mechanism and to provide safety for depositors. Competitive (or antitrust) policy, it was thought, had very limited applicability to banking because of its regulated character.[1]

Rather suddenly, competition in banking has emerged as an ostensibly relevant public policy consideration. What some have regarded as a "wave" of mergers and holding company formations is in part responsible.[2] Fears of monopoly and of a substantial lessening of competi-

Reprinted with permission from *The Journal of Finance*, Vol. XIX, No. 1 (March, 1964), pp. 32-45.

* This paper was prepared while the author was serving as a consultant to the Banking Markets Unit, Division of Research and Statistics, Board of Governors of the Federal Reserve System. The paper is not an official project of that Unit and the views expressed are those of the author. Thanks are due to Tynan Smith, George R. Hall and Robert C. Holland, all of the Board staff, and to James R. Schlesinger for many helpful comments.

† University of Pennsylvania.

[1] See, for example, Adolf A. Berle, "Banking Under the Antitrust Laws," *Columbia Law Review*, vol. 49 (1949). As recently as 1959, Carl Kaysen and Donald F. Turner classed commercial banks among those industries for which conventional antitrust policy was inapplicable. See their *Antitrust Policy: An Economic and Legal Analysis* (Cambridge, Mass., 1959), pp. 42-43, 291. For a brief discussion of regulations, see *National Banks and Future*, Report of the Advisory Committee on Banking to the Comptroller of the Currency (Washington, 1962).

[2] The recent "wave" has been an increasing one. In the 1940's, the average annual number was 81. For the period 1950-59, the average number was 150. Since the passage of the Bank Merger Act of 1960, the rate has been about 160 per year. These rates, however, are far below those of the late 1920's. See Charlotte P. and David A. Alhadeff, "Recent Bank Mergers," *Quarterly Journal of Economics*, vol. 69 (November, 1955); *Annual Report of the Comptroller of the Currency* (Washington, 1960); *Annual Report of the Federal Deposit Insurance Corporation* (Washington, 1960, 1961, 1962).

tion have arisen with regard to an industry which hitherto few had regarded as competitive in the first place. Congress responded with the Bank Holding Company Act of 1956 and the Banker Merger Act of 1960. The Department of Justice has brought Sherman and Clayton Act charges, and the courts—*because* of the regulations rather than *irrespective* of them—have found that commercial banking is to be treated as any other industry under the basic antitrust laws.[3]

In this paper, I shall argue on the one hand that commercial banking markets are typically not competitive enough to assure the efficient social performance of the industry. Evidence will be offered to demonstrate certain inefficiencies of the present banking structure which suggest the need for more intensive competition.

On the other hand, it will be contended that the existing complex of public policies with respect to banking, given the character of the industry, makes it quite impossible to achieve through conventional antitrust policies a type of competition which would be conducive to significantly improved performance. Public regulation and private organizational and institutional market characteristics make the performance of the industry insensitive to differences in market structure. As a result, orthodox policies aimed at maintaining or increasing competition by controlling the banking structure—as, for example, by preventing mergers —verge on the metaphorical "tilting at windmills." The performance of the industry will not be much affected by such policies so long as the regulatory and institutional characteristics remain unchanged.

The performance of banking markets could be improved, however. To achieve this, the most important changes in public policy would involve a relaxation of regulations and supervision to encourage more freedom of decision-making for *individual* banks, and to permit market forces to reward efficiency and to penalize inefficiency. The prohibition of such private competitive restraints as are inimical to the efficient functioning of the industry is also in order.

Paradoxically, it appears that, while the prevention of mergers cannot do much to maintain or increase competition, the increase in market rivalry signaled by changes in market organization would *foster* mergers and other types of consolidations. One of the virtually certain results of policies aimed at improving performance would be a slow but significant reduction in the number of banks in the country. This reduction in number would reduce the amount of inefficiency in banking but, because of the oligopolistic and locally-monopolistic structure of banking markets, because of remaining regulations, and because of the private organization of the industry, active price competition cannot and likely should not be achieved.

[3] *United States v. Philadelphia National Bank*, 374 U.S. 321 (1963). In addition several Sherman Act cases alleging conspiracy in restraint of trade have been brought.

The Evidence of Inadequate Competition

Competition is desirable because of its effects on market perform-ance and the allocation of scarce resources. Bankers, as is true of other businessmen, will not be persuaded by the academic scribbler who charges that competition does not prevail.[4] For to them—understand-ably—competition appears primarily as rivalry with other banks and finan-cial institutions and in concern over profits, market shares, and growth. The relationship between competition and efficient resources allocation is not their concern.

Assessing the degree of competition in a specific industry is typically difficult. With respect to commercial banking, however, the evidence is unusually persuasive, attesting really to the effectiveness of public policy in preventing the types of competition which would produce bank fail-ures and market instability. Thus, the principal evidence consists of: (1) the low failure rate and general stability in the structure of the industry; (2) the persistence of firms of less than the optimal scale; and (3) price performance which is inconsistent with the results of multi-lateral market competition.

Stability of the banking structure

During the ten years 1953-1963, there were only 91 voluntary bank liquidations and suspensions in an industry composed initially of about 14,000 firms.[5] Some of the liquidations may not have reflected adverse operating results. During the same period, there were 1,669 bank dis-appearances through mergers and absorptions, a small portion of which may have been motivated by "failing firm" considerations, but most of which occurred for other reasons. Thus, the rate of forced withdrawal from the banking industry has been remarkably low compared with other industries characterized by a large number of geographically dis-persed firms.[6] Banking has either been blessed with exceptionally able management which has prevented withdrawals due to shifts in market conditions, inefficiency and management errors or, more likely, has been afforded some shelter from dynamic market forces. Bank failure, in it-self, is of course not a goal of effective competition, but the risk of failure and, often, a turnover of firms are concomitants of competition. The

[4] For example, see the discussion of competition in *The Commercial Banking Industry*, American Bankers Association (New York, 1962), Ch. 1.

[5] "Changes in Banking Structure, 1953-62," *Federal Reserve Bulletin* (Septem-ber 1963).

[6] The rate of failure—and of new entrants—of retail and wholesale firms are many times this rate. For all industrial and commercial firms the failure rate is about 60 per month per 10,000 concerns.

higher bank failure rates prior to recent decades—and prior to extensive regulation and supervision—illustrate this point.[7]

The low failure rate is especially interesting in view of the size distribution of banks. Of the 12,933 insured commercial banks in existence at the end of 1962, 7,370 of them had total deposits of less than $5,000,000.[8] At the other extreme, only 314 banks had deposits of more than $100,000,000; 64 had deposits of over $500,000,000. The size distribution is highly skewed.

The same sort of distribution exists in many local and regional markets. In Chicago, for example, there were 154 banks in 1960, with the largest three having 48.1 per cent of total deposits. Similar figures for New York are 51 banks and 49.0 per cent; Philadelphia, 21 banks and 63.7 per cent; San Francisco, 18 banks and 50.6 per cent.[9] In these cities— and in many smaller ones—small banks frequently operate side-by-side with larger ones without apparent tendencies for the larger to force the smaller from the market. Larger banks, even without economics of scale, must possess some potential competitive advantage because of their greater assets and advantageous cross-elasticity of demand relationships. It would be expected, in other words, that without private or public sanctions moderating and rationalizing price rivalry, or without product differentiation sufficient to accomplish the same thing, there would tend to be more failures, especially among the smaller firms.

Scale economies

In effectively competitive markets, firms of less or greater than optimum scale are forced to make scale changes or to fail—though not necessarily in a short period of calendar time. It has become a commonplace, but certainly not an empirically proven fact, that there are economies of scale in banking.[10] In view of the conceptual difficulties involved in defining bank ouput, in treating product-mix and in separating the effects of branch and holding company operations in measuring scale, it is unlikely that the precise extent of these economies will be unearthed for some time to come. Nonetheless various estimates suggest that the economies are substantial up to at least $5,000,000 in deposits, and then perhaps plateau over size ranges up to the very largest of

---

[7] Anticipating a later argument, the consequences of these failures raises questions as to whether competition can be tolerated in banking.

[8] *Annual Report of the Federal Deposit Insurance Corporation* (1962), p. 134.

[9] Data developed in the Banking Markets Unit, Board of Governors of the Federal Reserve System, based on the principal county (or counties) of the cities, not on the entire S.M.S.A.

[10] David A. Alhadeff, Monopoly and Competition in Banking (Berkeley, 1954); Lyle E. Gramley, *Scale Economies in Banking* (Kansas City, 1962). But see also Paul Horvitz, "Economies of Scale in Banking," an unpublished paper for the Committee on Money and Credit, which questions the existence of economies of scale.

banks.[11] If it is true that economies extend only to the $5,000,000 deposit size, there would remain some 57 per cent of all commercial banks of less than optimal scale. If the economies extend to larger sizes, the percentage is even higher.

Such global figures may be misleading. In the first place, as of the end of 1962, 7,705 banks outside of metropolitan areas operated in one-bank towns.[12] Many of the smaller-than-optimum banks are found in this group. In some one-bank towns, the breadth of the market may be so restricted that the optimum scale cannot be achieved. Second, since the economies (or diseconomies) of branching operation and of the scale of branches are unknown, it could be argued that many of these small banks are still the most efficient of the alternatives practically available, and that no lack of competition is indicated.

This counter argument is not entirely convincing. While the breadth of the market in many towns may preclude even a single bank of optimum scale, competition would allow no more than one such bank. Yet, at the end of 1962, 1,800 banks operated in two-bank towns and 362 banks operated in three-bank towns.[13] Many of these banks are smaller than the apparent optimum, and market forces which foster the growth of one of them at the expense of the others are rarely observed. In addition, the fairly rapid development of branch operations in the wake of legislative changes in states such as Virginia and New York, and the premiums paid for the acquisition of small banks, especially where *de novo* entry is barred, are evidence that, at least in some types of operations, branch banking is more efficient than is unit banking.

Price behavior

For some industries, the behavior of prices is used as a prime indicator of the degree of competition. To be useful for this purpose, price data on individual transactions are typically necessary and very little of this sort of data is available for banks. The Federal Reserve's *Business Loan Surveys* of 1955-57 and its quarterly *Survey of Short-Term Business Loans* contain limited data on interest rates charged on individual commercial loans, but no full scale analysis of the competitive implications of these surveys has been released.[14] For rates on other types of loans, and for rates paid on time deposits, for checking account service charges, and other miscellaneous prices, all one has for individual banks is published announcements—from which there are frequent deviations—and collected personal experience.

[11] David A. Alhadeff, *op. cit.*
[12] "Changes in Banking Structure, 1953-62," *loc. cit.*
[13] *Ibid.*
[14] Reference is made below to some unpublished studies.

With these caveats, what can be said? First, it can be observed that individual banks charge different rates to different customers for what seem to be the same type and size of loan. These may be due in part to different risk factors and to other dimensions of the product being sold—the type of collateral, the timing of repayments, the amount of compensating balances required, etc. One gains the suspicion, however, that these factors would not account for the existing variance in rates,[15] and that the bank and individual customers are, in fact, in bilateral rather than openly competitive bargaining postures. The customer with the greater alternatives, including the alternative of not borrowing because of his excellent financial standing, is apt to get lower rates than the customer with fewer or no alternatives. To the extent that this is true, the bank can, within limits, operate as a discriminating monopolist.

The alternatives available to buyers would certainly be greater were they willing and able to "shop" among banks and other financial institutions for the best terms. If this occurred in substantial proportions, the variance in rates charged by individual banks for particular types of loans would tend to be small and there would tend to be only small differences in rates among banks in the same market. In other words, the monopoly power of sellers is inversely related to the ability of customers to "shop."

The data on interest rate variations within and among banks are indicative, yet not proof, of very little actual "shopping" by bank customers. To some extent it may be necessary for the bank-customer relationship to be a continuing one, but it also seems obvious that banks discourage their customers from seeking alternative sellers in ways which lower the effective cross-elasticity of demand among banks.[16] As a result, different banks in the same city are able to charge different rates for ostensibly identical loans. Price competition, which tends to generate uniform prices for the same product in a given market, is not very strong.

It is arguable that the lack of competition displayed by interest rates is a result of structural problems in the industry. With the conventional hypotheses of market theory, one would anticipate that rates would be somewhat lower and possess less variance in markets in which the number of banks is large, no one bank is of dominant size, and the distribution of size is not highly skewed. One might also conjecture that unit banks offer more attractive rates than do branch system and holding company banks if these forms of organization create or are associated with monopoly power.

[15] For example, rates charged on business loans of $1,000-$10,000 by a single bank at a given time ranged from 5 to 6.5 per cent according to the FRB quarterly *Survey of Short-Term Business Loans.*

[16] Cf. "Maintaining an Effective Bank Relationship," a speech by Charles A. Agemian before the 1963 Eastern Area Conference of the Financial Executives Institute, reported under "Required Reading," *American Banker* (August 5, 6, and 7, 1963).

There is little to support such hypotheses in banking markets. In a study of short-term loans to business by large banks in 19 major cities, the Banking Markets Unit, Board of Governors of the Federal Reserve System, has failed to find that market structure variables are associated with interest rates in any significant way. For small business loans ($1,000-$10,000)—a type of lending for which there are few alternatives outside of commercial banking—interest rates were found to vary significantly by the region of the country in which the cities covered by the study were located. After accounting for the regional effect, there was a slight but significant tendency for the rates charged by individual banks to decrease as the share of the market possessed by the bank increased.[17] The number of banks in the markets, the size of the largest bank, and the proportion of the market accounted for by the three largest banks, all possessed no explanatory value, even when checked for interaction effects.[18]

For large business loans ($200,000 and more), total variance in rates was found to be as large as that for the small loans. The regional influence was still significant—casting doubt on the idea that a truly national market exists for such loans. The larger banks tended to charge slightly but significantly lower rates than did the smaller banks. As with the small loans, the number of banks and the proportion of total deposits held by the three largest banks were not significant. There was no evidence that banks in a branching system charged rates different from those of unit banks.

[17] This may well be due to the larger banks selecting the higher quality loans.

[18] Mr. Frank Edwards, using data from the 1955 *Business Loan Survey*, reports a statistically significant but absolutely very small positive relationship between interest rates and concentration for 1955. Data for 1957 do not confirm this relationship. His study uses the average rate paid on business loans, including term loans, by city by asset size class of borrower as the dependent variable in a multiple correlation test. The study by the Banking Markets Unit uses the average rate paid on short-term business loans by bank by city. Variance in rates among banks within a city is thus included in the latter, but not on the Edwards study. It is possible that it is the inclusion of inter-bank as well as inter-city variances which causes concentration ratios to fail the tests of significance in the Banking Market Unit Study. If this is the reason for the difference in findings, the conclusions based on total variance including inter-bank, intra-city variance seems to be the better. Edwards argues that the null results for 1957 are due to a "ceiling effect" which reduces total variance during periods of high interest rates. This argument would be as valid for 1960, the time of the FRB study, as for 1957.

It is interesting to note that the Supreme Court, in *United States v. Philadelphia National Bank*, was willing to conclude from simple and untested structural hypotheses that performance improves as the number of banks increases. "Specifically, we think that a merger which produces a firm controlling an undue percentage share of the relevant market and results in a significant increase in the concentration of firms in that market, is so inherently likely to lessen competition substantially that it must be enjoined in the absence of evidence clearly showing that the merger is not likely to have such anticompetitive effects." The Court, relying on Kaysen and Turner, *op. cit.* and others, observed that "[C]ompetition is likely to be the greatest when there are many sellers, none of which has any significant market share" (374 U.S. 321, at 363).

Finally, in a smaller and admittedly less reliable study of small banks in several Minnesota towns, the Banking Markets Unit inquired into differences in interest rates depending on whether there were one, two or three banks in the town. The results indicated that the number of banks was unimportant in explaining rates charged even after the effects of loan mix, bank size, city size, level of income, and rate of change in city size and income were removed.[19] Interest rates paid on time deposits did not vary significantly with the number of commercial banks, but did tend to be higher in towns in which savings and loan associations were large relative to commercial banks. While neither rates charged nor rates paid varied significantly with size of bank, net earnings per dollar of earnings assets tended to increase slightly as the size of banks increased. Net earnings per dollar of earning assets tended to decrease as the number of banks increased, implying—since neither rates charged nor rates paid varied significantly with number of banks—that the competition associated with number of banks may result in higher costs rather than lower prices.

Public Regulation and Private Rationalization of Competition

The apparent lack of strong price competition, the continued existence of many banks of less than optimal scale and the insensitivity of market performance to market structure are not difficult to explain. They arise because of a vastly complex system of public regulation and supervision working in conjunction with a well-developed, yet generally informal, private market organization.[20] Most of the public regulation appears in the guise of instruments designed to protect the safety of banks and the liquidity of the payments mechanism—that is, to prevent bank failures and banking practices which might lead to failures. Much, but not all, of the private rationalization of competition is a side effect of certain cooperative arrangements among bankers—clearing houses, loan participations, and correspondent relations, for example—which add to the efficiency of the system. The point is not that there are conscious efforts to arrange conspiracies in restraint of trade, but rather that public regulation has the express purpose and private organization has the necessary effect of producing essentially non-competitive results.

Since public regulation is not pervasive of all facets of bank operations, and the private organization is typically informal, their restraining effects may not be obvious in those market areas in which the number of

---

[19] This is contrary to the findings of Irving Schweiger and John S. McGee, *Chicago Banking* (Chicago, 1961).

[20] See Donald R. Hodgman, *Commercial Bank Loan and Investment Policy* (Champaign, Illinois, 1963), pp. 158-160, for a similar view.

banks is reasonably large and there is such a lack of concentration that the possibility of strong leadership is absent. As already noted, however, a substantial portion of all commercial banks operate in communities in which there are no more than three banks. The relevant market of some of these banks undoubtedly extends to areas outside their own communities, thus making the effective number of banks in the market larger that the community count of banks indicates. Still, to the extent that the geographic market for any bank service contains only a small number of sellers, conventional oligopoly theory is relevant. Without formal agreement and without direct communication concerning prices to be charged and market areas and customers to be served, tacit understandings quite similar to those which would be achieved by overt agreement are apt to arise. In the case of banks, the tacit understandings—which, parenthetically, may not be consciously recognized as such by the participants—are abetted by public regulation and supervision which helps to assure that no individual bank will behave in a way which would have a strong competitive impact on others.[21]

Public regulation

Very little of the public regulation of banks positively requires identical pricing. The most obvious instances relate not to output prices—rates charged—but to the prices paid for inputs—rates paids for funds. Here regulations require that no interest be paid on demand deposits and establish an upper limit to interest paid on time deposits. Until recent years, the latter was low enough so that the maximum rate was also typically the actual rate, though this is no longer so generally true.[22]

Control of input prices may have profound effects on the degree of competition for output. There have been numerous instances in industrial markets in which an anti-competitive pricing system for output developed and was maintained through the control of input prices. The crux of the *Socony-Vacuum* case[23] was that major oil companies agreed to purchase "hot oil" and gasoline refined from this oil in an effort to prevent some of themselves and independent, non-integrated, companies from having significantly different costs. Without the condition of equal costs, the tacit agreement to follow the output price leadership of Standard of Indiana tended chronically to breakdown. Other cases in which cost identity was

---

[21] See *ibid.*, pp. 116-135, 159-160, for an excellent discussion of the "administered" and oligopolistically set New York prime rate and its effects in restraining competition. See also David C. Motter, "Bank Mergers and Public Policy," *National Banking Review*, vol. 1 (September, 1963), p. 96, especially fn. 23.

[22] See Caroline H. Cagle, "Interest Rates on Time Deposits, Mid-February 1963," *Federal Research Bulletin* (June 1963).

[23] *United States v. Socony-Vacuum Oil Co.*, 310 U.S. 150 (1940).

important in rationalizing output competition can be found in the beet sugar,[24] milk distribution,[25] and cigarette[26] industries.

In banking, it would be unwarranted to conclude that the regulation of interest paid on deposits creates a tight system of collusive output prices. However, they have—purposely—been instrumental in the general moderation of competition. The regulations prevent considerable price competition for funds, both among banks and between banks and other financial institutions. One consequence has been the prevention of what would otherwise have been a form of cost-increasing rivalry for funds and, for this reason, the erection of a protective shield for the less efficient and often smaller banks. In addition, the lack of competition for funds has been an important ingredient in eliminating cost differences which, especially in local markets, would be apt to get translated into more active competition in the output market. Banks, being unable to attract customers by paying higher rates on deposits, have had no alternative but to use non-price forms of rivalry. The resulting product differentiation—based on location, convenience, advertising, loan accommodations, etc.—have likely reduced the desire and ability of customers to shop among banks. The expenses involved in advertising and the proliferation of branches may in some instances have resulted in higher bank operating costs than would prevail with more rate competition. Moreover, since even the most aggressive banks have been restricted in their ability to use deposit rates as a competitive weapon, tacit understandings to compete only with non-price techniques are made more viable. In short, the regulations tend to create more identical "value systems" among banks and, hence, to prevent the outbreak of open price rivalry.[27]

Similar tendencies for an identity of value systems arise from other aspects of regulation. Only a few of the regulations go directly to prices and terms for deposits and loans. Most have a more subtle effect. Limitations on mortgage lending and ownership of stocks, along with supervisory rules governing the risk asset ratio, standards for lending, and for accounting procedures, make for similar asset compositions and for similar views with respect to "sound" banking practices. Bankers, that is, are encouraged to conform to an established and, in many respects, noncompetitive pattern of market behavior.

Finally, state and Federal regulations prevent various forms of entry into the markets of existing banks. Whether nationally or state chartered, banks cannot establish branches across state lines even though

[24] *Mandeville Island Farms, Inc. v. American Crystal Sugar Co.* 334 U.S. 219 (1948).

[25] *Pevely Dairy Co. v. United States*, 178 F.2d 363 (8th Cir. 1949).

[26] *American Tobacco Co. v. United States*, 328 U.S. 781 (1946).

[27] For a more complete discussion of the role of differences in costs and other aspects of "value systems" of firms on competition, see Almarin Phillips, *Market Structure, Organization and Performance* (Cambridge, Mass. 1962) pp. 32-40.

the economic market does not accord with these political boundaries. With respect to both entry by new banks and entry by existing banks through merger or *de novo* branching, the "adequacy" of the existing banks to meet the convenience and needs of the market is considered. The question of convenience and needs of a market very often reduces to the question of whether existing banks would be injured if they shared their market with another, not to whether there are economic reasons for the establishment of a new bank. These regulations facilitate tacit market sharing and reduce the likelihood that "maverick" bankers—those who might upset the status quo of a market—will enter.

The entry problem is a more difficult one in banking than in other industries, however. Entry performs its valuable role in allocating resources efficiently because of its effects on long-run supply. While in local markets a new bank may increase supply and tend to force down prices (if the new bank does not adopt the same non-competitive behavior of the existing banks), in the aggregate the total supply of bank credit is loosely fixed by monetary authority. For the entire economy, more banks do not mean a larger total supply in the same sense as is the case in other industries, or in the same sense as they do for local and regional bank markets. Rather, if the number of banks increases and supply of bank credit is fixed, the size of the average bank decreases and, assuming the existence of scale economies, the system moves away from the most efficient allocation of resources. If the competitive force of new entrants is to be relied upon to achieve efficiency, free entry in banking must take the two-way meaning attached to it in competitive theory— freedom of entrance and freedom of exit (failure or forced disappearance through merger). Forced exit, of course, is precisely what regulation and supervision, including restrictions on entry, are designed to prevent. As a result, the banking structure has responded very slowly to inefficient operations and to geographical shifts in demand.

Private organization

Public regulation is not the only source of rationalized competition among banks. It may not be even the primary source. The rationalization which comes from the organizational and institutional aspects of banks themselves is more difficult to see but probably no less important.

The informal organization of oligopoly in local markets was mentioned above. There are also several more formal types of horizontal relations. Of these, the clearing house is the most familiar. Its function of clearing balances is a necessary one, but one which does not require either the ownership of or active participation in the clearing house by the member banks. The functions beyond those of clearing which are performed are something of a mystery to any save the members, but no one would be surprised if matters such as hours of business, service charges on checking accounts, and perhaps even interest rates charged and paid, were occasionally discussed.

Commercial banking, as other industries, has its trade associations—local, regional, state and nationwide bankers associations. These associations undoubtedly perform valuable informational and educational services. They also provide a forum for communication among bankers and an opportunity for those high in the organizational hierarchy—the leaders of the industry—to make known their views on sundry subjects. This sort of communication can hardly result in formal conspiracy among bankers; there are too many members in the group, the subject matter is too complex, and the disciplinary power is too weak. Still, the associations have their purpose. When problems arise, established channels of communication are available. And communication, especially when it comes from those at the top of a power hierarchy, tends to facilitate conflict resolution. Perhaps a great deal should not be made of this, but competition is a form of conflict and, in the present context, conflict resolution is a form of restraint on competition. If nothing more, the communication makes it easier to know what is expected of a "good" banker; easier to conform to "sound" banking practice.

In addition to horizontal relations there is in the organization of banking an explicit vertical relationship among banks. It is found in correspondent banking. It is well-recognized that a system of vertical affiliations among firms may restrain competition. This is probably one effect of correspondent banking, but the restraint is perhaps a mild one. Unlike resale price maintenance, in which the vertical relations may operate in a manner identical to that which would occur with full horizontal agreement among distributors, correspondent relations exert a less obvious influence. There is no commodity flowing from the correspondent to corresponding bank which is resold. And it is general practice that the several banks in one community correspond with different banks in others.

The correspondent system tends to pyramid from a large number of banks in small cities and towns upward to a smaller number of banks in a few larger cities and upward again to a small number of banks in one or a few financial centers. Detailed knowledge of the full role played by correspondent banks is lacking and generalizations are hazardous. It is known that corresponding comprises much more than a holding of deposit balances and a clearing operation. Services and information flow from correspondents to the corresponding banks, in a direction opposite to that of the deposits. These often include advice with respect to portfolio, credit advice, and a sort of management consulting service. There are, in addition, loan participations which alter the otherwise vertical relation to a horizontal one.

To reiterate, this does not completely foreclose competition. But, as argued above, the banks in each of the cities involved have an implicitly recognized community of interest which arises from their horizontal and frequently oligopolistic market relations. Even while banks in one town generally correspond with different banks in the city at the next level up, the horizontal relations at each level are such as to produce substantial uniformity of behavior. The correspondent relations provide another system of communication among banks and easy access to information which allows and encourages all the banks in the system to conform to established modes of behavior.

The unique combination of formal and informal organization in commercial banking—partly associated with public regulation and supervision and partly with private, institutional arrangements—explains the lack of competitive market performance and the failure of that performance to vary with the market structure. This organization is by far the most pervasive factor in determining performance. "Good" banking practices are equated with "quiet," non-price forms of rivalry in the view of both bankers and the regulatory agencies.

Improving Commercial Banking Performance

It would be possible and, within limits, it probably is desirable to improve the performance of commercial banking markets. It appears, however, that the role of conventional antitrust policy—the prevention of mergers and combinations in restraint of trade—in achieving this result is an extremely limited one, because of the continuing necessity for some public regulation and supervision and also because of the impossibility of altering substantially the oligopolistic structure of the typical banking market.

The most obvious need for public intervention is to preserve the liquidity of the money supply which, in the absence of deposit insurance, requires supervision and regulations to prevent bank failures. With deposit insurance, the liquidity of the payments mechanism depends not on the liquidity and solvency of the banks themselves, but rather on the liquidity of those to whom the banks owe debts—the depositors—which it is the function of the insurance to maintain. Nonetheless, deposit insurance does not make possible the elimination of bank regulation and supervision. If the insuring agency did no more than examine banks for the purpose of discriminating in premiums on the basis of risk, *de facto* regulations would continue to exist. Moreover, given the highly leveraged position of bank capital and the liquidity of bank liabilities, continued supervision and regulation will be necessary to prevent systematic failures and their generally disrupting influence.

Regulation, then, will continue, but the nature of regulation requires modification. If it is accepted that the organization, rather than the structure, of the industry is the controlling variable in determining performance, it follows that the primary means of altering performance is through changing the organization, especially that part which emanates from regulations.

The most important single policy would be to permit freer entry. This would involve making new charters available on a less restrictive basis than is done on the current "needs and convenience" criterion, removing arbitrary limitations on *de novo* branching and branching by merger, and ending the prohibitions against branching over state lines. Efficient independent banks and those smaller banks which offer differential services for which there is market demand would not be forced from the market by these changes. Inefficient banks would have to improve their efficiency, merge, or fail; the market power of locally monopolistic or oligopolistic banks would be effectively constrained.

The elimination of restrictions on interest rates paid on deposits would be another important step. This, especially if accompanied by steps to equalize the reserve requirements of all banks, regardless of size,[28] would remove what amounts to protective subsidization of smaller banks. In addition, bank supervision could be modified to permit banks greater freedom in establishing their own credit and risk standards. Increased price competition would not likely arise from permitting banks to experiment with new types of credit or to specialize in particular lines, but there would be encouragement for a constructive type of non-price competition. Competition through advertising, promotion, and location would to some degree be supplanted by competition through new and improved loan and deposit services.

The removal of interest rate restrictions and the relaxation of regulations would also tend to reduce the number of banks. The increased cost of funds, while good for the industry as a whole and its relations with other financial institutions, would tend to increase operating costs. Some banks, because of the cost increase and because of management errors in the extension of credit, would experience operating difficulties; some would fail, perhaps to be absorbed by another bank or to be succeeded by a new firm.

These are not small changes in policy. Accomplishing them would require the establishment of a *national* policy for what should be a *national* industry. Uniform chartering and branching policies, uniform and less compulsory supervisory standards, uniform reserve requirements and free interstate banking would spell the end of the dual banking system as it now exists. Moreover, while the social benefits appear to merit such changes, they are radical enough to suggest that they should be accomplished in small steps over a period of years. The opposition

---

[28] Including for this purpose interbank deposits and vault cash in reserves.

of bankers to the proposals probably is assurance that no change will be rapid!

Finally, some sort of antitrust policy would still be necessary. While clearing houses, loan participations and correspondent relationships are necessary to the industry, there is no obvious reason why other horizontal and vertical combinations in restraint of trade should be accorded special Sherman Act exemption. That is, the private organization of the industry should be left intact except where it has no purpose other than to restrain trade. A necessary caution here is that the sometimes extremely difficult distinction must be made between those kinds of cooperative endeavors which are necessary because of the character and structure of the industry—and, hence, are "reasonable" restraints—and those which are unnecessary and operate to the detriment of society. This calls for the antitrust standard used by Judge Medina in the *Morgan* case[29] rather than the usual *per se* procedures for restraint of trade cases. Too, it should be recognized in antitrust proceedings that the classical type of atomistic competition cannot be made to prevail in banking markets. The most that can be sought is oligopolistic competition for differentiated products, constrained by freedom of entry and the ability of existing banks to innovate.

Similarly, while legislative barriers to mergers should be removed to encourage competition, competitive policy for the industry should, at the same time, include the prohibition of mergers and holding companies which may tend to lessen competition substantially. This is a difficult standard to apply, however, and even when enforcement is in the antitrust agencies—as it should be—rather than lodged with regulatory authorities, there is danger that the policy could evolve into the protection of small and inefficient competitors rather than a policy to promote competition.[30] An extremely strict merger policy would make it difficult to realize scale economics and the benefits of freer entry.

---

[29] *United States v. Morgan*, 118 F. Supp. 621 (S.D.N.Y. 1954).

[30] It can be argued that the trend of enforcement of the amended Section 7 of the Clayton Act has already turned in this direction. In particular, see *Brown Shoe v. United States*, 370 U.S. 294 (1962). *United States v. Philadelphia National Bank*, 374 U.S. 321 (1963) may have similar overtones despite the testimony of small bankers that they favored the merger. A more competitive market environment could easily alter their views.

2

Stimulating bank competition through regulatory action

*Paul M. Horvitz**

In recent years there have been many proposals for legislation to stimulate competition among financial institutions. There have been extensive legislative proposals made by the Commission on Money and Credit, by the President's Committee on Financial Institutions, and by the Advisory Committee to the Comptroller of the Currency.[1] In a recent article in this journal Almarin Phillips advanced several proposals for legislation to stimulate banking competition.[2] These and other studies have led to the introduction of a large number of bills in Congress relating to banking.[3]

Very few of these bills, and none of the significant ones, have been enacted into law. As our past history has demonstrated, it is very difficult to get significant legislation pertaining to financial institutions through Congress in the absence of a financial crisis. Because the prospects for legislative action in the near future are not very great, it is

Reprinted with permission from *The Journal of Finance*, Vol. XX, No. 1 (March, 1965), pp. 1-13.

* The author is Senior Economist, Office of the Comptroller of the Currency. The views expressed in this paper are those of the author. He is grateful to Weldon Welfling, Benjamin Klebaner, and his colleagues in the Office of the Comptroller of the Currency for many helpful comments.

[1] *Money and Credit*. Report of the Commission on Money and Credit (Englewood Cliffs, N.J.: Prentice-Hall, Inc., 1961); *Report of the Committee on Financial Institutions* (Washington: U.S. G.P.O., 1963); *National Banks and the Future*, Report of the Advisory Committee on Banking to the Comptroller of the Currency (Washington: U.S. G.P.O., 1962).

[2] "Competition, Confusion, and Commercial Banking," *Journal of Finance*, March 1964.

[3] For a list of the bills pending before Congress in mid-1964, see *American Banker*, June 22, 1964, P. 7.

worthwhile to investigate the possibilities for stimulating competition among financial institutions through action of the regulatory authorities. The purpose of this paper is to consider some of the actions that have been taken and which could be taken by the various supervisory agencies (without new legislation) to stimulate competition among commercial banks, and between commercial banks and other financial institutions.

I. Banking Structure

Probably the most important area for regulatory action by the banking supervisory agencies lies in the field of bank chartering, branching, and bank mergers. An increase in entry by new banks is clearly one of the most effective ways of stimulating competition in banking.[4] In recent years there has been some discussion of the desirability of easing entry into banking; these discussions have even gone to the extent of considering "free banking," a subject which had been thought dead for many years.[5]

1. Chartering

The major regulatory barrier to new entry is heavy reliance on what Alhadeff calls "the need doctrine." Under present procedures, a new bank is chartered only if the community "needs" a new bank. The major reason for rejection of applications for new entry by national banks has been "insufficient need."[6] There is, of course, no clear criterion of what constitutes sufficient need. When a charter application is rejected on grounds of "insufficient need" or "unfavorable earnings prospects," the chartering authorities are in effect substituting their judgement for that of the applicants. A considerable easing of entry would result from a decision of the chartering authorities to refrain from overruling the judgement of the people risking their capital on the new bank.

In many cases "insufficient need" really means that there is insufficient demand to support comfortably the existing banks plus a new bank. This decision fundamentally involves the degree of risk of bank failure we are willing to tolerate to gain a more competitive banking structure, since it is likely that freer entry and more competition in banking would

[4] Phillips argues that "[t]he most important single policy [to improve performance] would be to permit freer entry." *Op. cit.*, p. 44.

[5] See, for example, David Alhadeff, "A Reconsideration of Restrictions on Bank Entry," *Quarterly Journal of Economics*, May 1963; Donald P. Jacobs, "The Framework of Commercial Bank Regulation: An Appraisal," *The National Banking Review*, March 1964; and David C. Motter and Deane Carson "Bank Entry and the Public Interest: A Case Study," *National Banking Review*, June 1964.

[6] See Bernard Shull and Paul Horvitz, "Branch Banking and the Structure of Competition," *National Banking Review*, March 1964, Tables 4 and 5.

lead to more bank failures. Attitudes on this issue vary. There are those who hold that bank failures are disastrous and we should at all costs keep the number of failures as close to zero as possible. This approach can be found in statements by state banking supervisors to the Joint Economic Committee in 1952. For example, the Oregon supervisor stated that:[7]

I do not believe that . . . I should approve a second bank . . . where it seems evident that the existing bank would be weakened by the loss of a portion of the existing business.

Along the same lines, the California supervisor argued that "competition is not a reasonable public necessity in the case of banking,"[8] and the Connecticut supervisor stated that "[s]ound and ethical competition is . . . a healthy thing but, of course, not to the extent of hazard to existing independent banking institutions."[9] Most other state banking supervisors made similar responses.

However, it is by no means clear that bank failures are necessarily the disaster they are commonly considered to be. The failure of the textile mill in the one-mill New England town is almost certainly a greater community disaster than the failure of the local bank in a one-bank town. Of course, an epidemic of bank failures such as we have experienced in the past is to be avoided, but with the existence of federal deposit insurance a few bank failures need not lead to disaster to any community or to a wave of bank runs or failures. Much concern has been expressed over the failure of five banks in the first eight months of 1964, although losses to depositors were small and in no sense had a calamitous effect on the local economy. In contrast to the five bank failures out of over 13,000 banks in operation, we might note that during this same period business failures were at an annual rate of about 55 per 10,000 concerns. Obviously bank failures are not desirable, but failures may be symptomatic of vigorous competition, and vigorous competition *is* desirable.

In addition to the need criterion, another regulatory restriction on entry concerns management of the proposed bank. "Unsatisfactory management" has been an important reason for rejection of applications for new national bank charters. Chartering authorities put heavy weight on the background and character of the proposed bank's management and directors. There is no information available to indicate the basis on which the authorities separate the "good guys" from the "bad guys." It is not impossible that those charter applicants whose backgrounds and expe-

[7] Joint Committee on the Economic Report, *Monetary Policy and the Management of the Public Debt*, 82d Cong., 2d Sess. 1952, P. 994.

[8] *Ibid.*, p. 995.

[9] *Ibid.*, p. 990.

rience indicate a tendency toward vigorous competition and price cutting may be classified with the "bad guys."[10]

The present Comptroller of the Currency has taken a more liberal attitude with respect to applications for new national bank charters than some of his predecessors, and this seems to have had a stimulating effect also on actions by state chartering authorities. It has also led to an increase in applications for new bank charters. Obscured by the controversy which this policy has generated is the fact that the number of new banks chartered each year is still not very high. Only 164 national banks were chartered *de novo* in 1963. While this is a large number in comparison with the 26 chartered in 1961 it does not seem strikingly large when compared with the more than 4,600 national banks in existence.

Many bankers and banking organizations have been upset by this increase in chartering activity, as is to be expected. One of their complaints, however, is interesting. They charge that there has been a breakdown in coordination between Federal and State chartering authorities. The coordination they refer to is the practice that apparently prevailed in the past of allocating territories between national and state chartered banks so as not to provide any substantial increase in competition for the existing banks through issuance of new charters.

2. Branching

Competition can also be stimulated by new entry through branching. There has been an increase in branching activity where it is authorized by law in recent years. Again it is important that applications for new branches be evaluated on their merits and not on the basis of any sort of territorial or numerical allocations among the supervisory agencies. In this area, also, there have been claims of a breakdown in coordination between federal and state regulatory agencies. Part of this coordination involves the concept of priority. As Llewellyn Brown, Mississippi State Comptroller has put it: "There has always been an informal understanding between the supervisors and the Comptroller that in competitive application situations, and all other factors being equal, priority would be given to the application filed first."[11] In practice, the policy of "priority" meant that once a bank filed an application for a branch in a particular community, it could rest assured that no competing bank could estab-

---

[10] Reuben Kessel has discussed the way in which restrictions on entry into medicine operate to discourage or discriminate against those who may become price-cutting doctors. See his "Price Discrimination in Medicine," *The Journal of Law and Economics*, October 1958, esp. pp. 46-50.

[11] Llewellyn Brown, State Comptroller, Mississippi, *Conflict of Federal and State Banking Laws*, Hearings Before the Committee on Banking and Currency, House of Representatives, 88th Congress, First Session, 1963, p. 200.

lish a branch in that community first. There was then no hurry to provide the additional branch facilities applied for.

Recent hearings before the House Banking and Currency Committee provided an excellent example of this practice:[12]

> **Mr. Brown.** Canton, Miss. is a small agricultural town of 9,700 people located in the center of my State. There are two banks there, the Canton Exchange Bank, a State bank, and the First National Bank.
>
> On April 16, 1962, I received a letter from Mr. J. D. Gwin, the chief national bank examiner of the Sixth Federal Reserve District, indicating the receipt of an application from the First National Bank to establish a branch in the neighboring community of Ridgeland. . . .
>
> . . . I replied by stating that the Canton Exchange Bank had an application on file to open a branch in Ridgeland and that I was in the process of approving that application. I might state that the Canton Exchange Bank application had been on file since August of 1961 and that we had been discussing the matter for some time before that. Frankly, I thought my letter would end the matter. . . .
>
> . . . The next thing I knew about this matter was informal advice from the Canton Exchange Bank that the application of the First National Bank had been granted. The application of the Canton Exchange Bank had already been granted by me. The result, therefore, is two branches in a location which, in my view, can only support one branch. . . .
>
> **Mr. St. Germain.** You cite the Canton Exchange Bank, that an application had been filed since August of 1961. Is it not a fact that this particular one was pending since 1957?
>
> **Mr. Brown.** True, sir. I didn't think you would be interested in going back too far. . . .

It appears that in this case the state supervisor had a branch application since 1957. No action was taken on the application until a branch of a national bank in the community became a possibility. Collusive arrangements among the supervisors to bar entry are just as serious as collusive practices among the banks and should not be allowed to continue even if masked as "coordination" or "cooperation."

New branches can be authorized under existing interpretations of branching laws in some states and also by reconsidering the restrictions on branching which exist in others. Federal law restricts national bank branches in any state to the same geographic limitations which apply to state banks under the laws of that state. Many of these state laws are not clear as to the geographical limitations on branching privileges of state banks. Previous policy of the Office of the Comptroller of the Currency seems to have been that branches would not be approved for national banks unless the state law was clear-cut in authorizing branches

[12] *Ibid.*, pp. 199, 200, 234.

in certain areas. Present policy seems to be that branches will be approved for national banks where, under a reasonable interpretation of the state law, it is not forbidden.

An example may be the Michigan law which does not allow a bank to establish a branch in any "village" in which a bank is already operating. The law does not define "village." This leaves to the chartering authority the decision as to whether a proposed branch will be located in the same village as an existing bank. Another example of a state law subject to diverse interpretation is that of Virginia. Virginia allows branching statewide if and only if the branch is acquired by merger. The question has been raised as to whether such procedural restrictions bind the Comptroller in his decisions or whether he is bound only by the *geographical* limitations of state law.

Obviously, a policy of making decisions in such cases can and has led to some litigation of disputed interpretations of the law.[13] This seems to be perfectly appropriate under our judicial system. Differences of opinion as to interpretation of law should be settled in the courts, rather than through the decision of a regulatory authority to avoid controversy and lawsuits by adopting an overly restrictive policy on approval of new branches.

3. Mergers

Probably the most important decisions of regulatory authorities which affect competition in banking are those with respect to bank mergers. Under the Bank Merger Act of 1960, a merger resulting in an insured bank must be approved in advance by either the Comptroller of the Currency, the Federal Reserve Board, or the FDIC, depending on whether the resulting bank is a national, state member, or non-member insured bank. Of course, not all bank mergers are undesirable. By most standards there are too many small, inefficient banks operating in the United States. It is clear that whatever the general policy on bank mergers may be, over the long run the tendency is going to be toward reduction in the number of these small banks.[14] The Bank Merger Act requires

[13] Among the cases which have led to litigation are: *Manufacturers National Bank of Detroit v. James J. Saxon and Community National Bank of Pontiac*, Civil Action No. 25172 (D.C. E.D. Mich.); *W. M. Jackson v. First National Bank of Valdosta*, Civil Action No. 647 (D.C. M.D. Ga.); *Manufacturers National Bank of Detroit v. James J. Saxon and Michigan Bank, N. A.*, Civil Action No. 2460 (D.C. E.D. Mich.); *North Madison Bank v. National Bank of Madison, Indiana, and James J. Saxon*, Civil Action No. NA 63-C-76 (D.C. S.D. Ind. 1963). For a summary of the issues in pending cases, see each issue of *The National Banking Review*.

[14] In fact, as Phillips has pointed out, a policy of freer entry coupled with the Federal Reserve restriction of the aggregate amount of bank credit would lead to a reduction in the average size of banks in the absence of exit by some banks. If there are economies of scale in banking, merger is a relatively painless way of eliminating firms too small to be efficient. Phillips, *op. cit.*, p. 41.

that the appropriate regulatory agency weigh the impact of the merger on competition along with the so-called banking factors (financial history of the banks, adequacy of capital, character of management, etc.). Many economists and some lawmakers have complained that the regulatory agencies do not give sufficient weight to the competitive factor.[15]

It is not easy to determine how much weight is given to the competition factor by the regulatory authorities in making merger decisions. George Hall and Charles Phillips have attempted to make such a determination by careful analysis of published merger decisions.[16] Hall and Phillips recognized the limitations[17] of their approach, but came to the general conclusion that competition as defined by economists is not the most important consideration:[18]

> The Federal banking authorities share a common approach to their duties under the Bank Merger Act of 1960. . . . Great stress is placed on the advantages to customers from the creation of larger banking organizations. . . . All three regard mergers as justified to neutralize the power of large banks. Conversely they all regard the existence of other large banks as protection against the misuse of market power stemming from a merger.
>
> . . . Increases in concentration as a result of a merger are regarded as a necessary price to pay to increase the availability of local banking services.

Part of the explanation for this may lie in the tendency within the supervisory agencies to have preliminary investigation of merger applications made by personnel connected with the bank examination function. Because of the close association of these people in their daily work with problems of bank safety, they may tend to give heavy emphasis to the strengthening aspects of bank mergers. Examiners may sincerely view the strengthening of the bank that results from a bank merger as increasing its ability to compete, and hence they may regard virtually all mergers as strengthening competition.

[15] See, for example, papers on the Supreme Court's decision in the Philadelphia National Bank case by Edward S. Herman, Thomas G. Moore in *The National Banking Review*, March 1964, and by Emmanuel Celler, December 1963. On the other hand, the President's Committee on Financial Institutions concluded that: "The effect on competition, although it is only one of seven factors specified in the Bank Merger Act, is accorded substantial weight." (*Report of the Committee on Financial Institutions*, p. 48).

[16] George R. Hall and Charles F. Phillips, Jr., *Bank Mergers and the Regulatory Agencies* (Washington: Board of Governors of the Federal Reserve System, 1964).

[17] The published decisions do not give a full picture of decisions regarding mergers. Some merger applications are discouraged and consequently withdrawn prior to a decision. Thus figures on the percentage of merger applications approved are not completely accurate. They concede that "[i]t is common knowledge that some aspects of merger cases may not always be expressed in print." A more important shortcoming may have been their presumption that there is, somewhere behind the published decisions, a reasoned, rational merger policy in the minds of the regulatory authorities. The published merger decisions demonstrate more inconsistency than Hall and Phillips indicate.

[18] *Ibid.*, pp. 156, 158.

It had been true until quite recently at all three federal regulatory agencies that the merger application proceeded through bank examination and legal channels exclusively. Now, at the Federal Reserve and the Office of the Comptroller of the Currency, economists are involved at some stage in reviewing merger applications. These procedures, however, do not seem to have had much effect on decisions. It is rather the activities of the Justice Department which may lead to more weight being given to competitive factors in future merger decisions.

The emergence of the Justice Department as an important factor in bank mergers deserves some comment. The Bank Merger Act allows other factors to be taken into consideration in addition to the effect on competition and, of course, many mergers are justifiable and desirable on consideration of these banking factors.[19] It was inevitable, however, that the Justice Department would seek influence and control over bank merger decisions because, in terms of anti-trust concepts, the regulatory authorities in the past have not given sufficient stress to competitive factors. Judging from the comments on the Philadelphia merger decision, it appears that most academic economists favor applying the anti-trust laws to banking.[20] Probably there would be less support among economists for applying the anti-trust laws to banking if, for example, Governor Robertson had been the sole decision-maker in bank merger cases—that is, if the decision-makers under the Bank Merger Act were more antagonistic to merger proposals.[21]

II. Price Competition

1. Regulation Q

Apart from matters of banking structure, the regulatory authorities can also play a significant role in promoting or allowing more price competition among banks. One of the most serious limitations on the ability of commercial banks to compete on a price basis with one another and with other financial institutions is the Federal Reserve Board's Regulation, which limits the rate of interest which may be paid by member banks on time deposits. The FDIC has a similar regulation applying to insured non-member banks. The best thing that could be done with

[19] A bank may have management problems that can best be solved by merger. Merger may be the best solution for banks in a declining community. Some mergers that reduce competition may be desirable to provide larger banking units in areas in which *de novo* branching is prohibited.

[20] See the references cited in footnote 15 and also "Competition, Confusion and Commercial Banking," p. 45.

[21] Governor Robertson dissented from the Board of Governors majority on 21 of the 46 mergers approved by the Board from January, 1963 to December, 1964. He was absent and did not vote in five of these approvals.

Regulation Q is simply to eliminate it. Banks should be allowed to compete for time deposits on a price basis, with the efficient banks paying higher rates and perhaps with some of the less efficient banks falling by the wayside.

Short of abolishing Regulation Q, the next best solution would be to put Regulation Q on a stand-by basis. This proposal has been made by the Commission on Money and Credit, the President's Committee on Financial Institutions, and the Comptroller's Advisory Committee. Supporters of the proposal feel that the Federal Reserve should have the power to impose ceilings paid on time deposits if it should become necessary, but they have not yet been able to spell out the circumstances under which it would be desirable to impose such ceilings.

Legislation is required either to eliminate Regulation Q or to put it on a stand-by basis, but even if no basic legislative change is made it is still possible to secure the desired result simply by raising the present ceiling to a point where it becomes inoperative. That is, with the ceiling now set at 4 per cent some banks are precluded from competing on a price basis for time deposits. If the ceiling were raised to, say, 6 per cent, there would be no banks which would be limited as to the interest they could pay by the ceiling.[22]

The principal justification for Regulation Q is the fear that competition for time deposits on a rate basis may lead banks to "reach" for unsound assets and thereby lead to a wave of bank failures.[23] It is frequently alleged that this occurred during the 1920's. There is, however, no evidence to support this. In fact, rates paid on time deposits by member banks *declined* during the 1920's.[24] Furthermore, as Anderson has pointed out, commercial banks maintained their holdings of U.S. government securities at 10 percent of total earning assets from 1920 to 1929.[25] This indicates an attempt on the part of banks to maintain the proportion of high quality assets in their portfolios.

There is not adequate data to answer the questions raised about the tendency of banks under competitive pressure during the 1920's to reach for unsound assets. Alhadeff has concluded that fears of deteriora-

---

[22] It should be mentioned that there is some doubt as to the power of the Federal Reserve to take such action. The Federal Reserve argues that the law requires the Board to set a meaningful ceiling. Nevertheless, it is clearly within their right to set a ceiling which will affect only a small number of banks.

[23] There is one other important justification for Regulation Q. The ceiling probably increases bank earnings over what they would be in the absence of the ceiling. The majority of bankers probably are in favor of retaining Regulation Q, and both the Federal Reserve and Congress seem to give weight to the views of the banks in such matters.

[24] See Paul S. Anderson, "A Note on Time Deposit Theory and Practice," *The National Banking Review*, March 1964, pp. 388-9.

[25] *Ibid.*

tion in the quality of bank assets in response to increased competition are exaggerated.[26]

One other aspect of Regulation Q should be mentioned. Under the definitions promulgated by the Federal Reserve Board under Regulation Q, corporations cannot hold savings deposits. This means that commercial banks cannot compete with one another and with savings and loan associations for this segment of time deposit business (except through the somewhat clumsy device of certificates of deposit). This is an important part of the market, not only because of its size but also because corporate savings depositors would probably be the most interest-sensitive segment of the market. If banks had to consider this group in their pricing decisions, the whole time deposit business could become more competitive. Again this is a step that can be taken by administrative ruling rather than requiring legislation.[27]

In view of the failure of the Federal Reserve to loose the bind of Regulation Q, it is not surprising that various means of legally evading the regulation have been devised. The sale of commercial paper by commercial banks is a promising development of this sort.

2. Service charges

Another area in which price competition could be stimulated is in the area of service charges on checking accounts. Until recently many local clearing houses had apparently set service charges on checking accounts to be charged by their members. Recent action by the Justice Department and the banking regulatory agencies, culminating in the conviction on price fixing charges of several banks in Minnesota, has greatly reduced this overt setting of prices. It is still not clear, however, whether collusion in the setting of service charges has been completely eliminated or simply driven underground. National Bank Examiners have been instructed to examine the service charge structure of national banks to determine that charges are established independently. While there are difficulties in making such a determination, the banks have learned that such practices are not acceptable banking procedure. There may still be

[26] "A Reconsideration of Restrictions on Bank Entry," pp. 256-260. See also George Benston, "Interest Payments on Demand Deposits and Bank Investment Behaviour," *Journal of Political Economy*, October 1964.

[27] The Comptroller of the Currency has ruled that "a national bank may, subject to withdrawal requirements and interest rate limitations imposed by applicable regulations, accept savings accounts without regard to whether the funds deposited are to the credit of one or more individuals, or of a corporation, association, or other organization, whether operated for profit or otherwise." (*Comptrollers Manual for National Banks*, 1964, Regulations § 7.9.) Federal Reserve opposition to this ruling has probably kept the number of banks accepting corporate savings accounts small.

collusive arrangements among banks in which clearing houses play a prominent role. Business hours are one possible example.[28]

Obviously, all conspiracies to fix prices can and should be eliminated. Apart from actual conspiracy, however, tacit collusion is still a problem. Professor Phillips has argued that tacit collusion is a more serious problem in banking than in most other industries. This is due not only to the small number of competing banks in most market areas, but also to the existence of a structure of public regulation that "has the express purpose . . . of producing essentially non-competitive results." Phillips notes that:[29]

> Without formal agreement and without direct communication concerning prices to be charged and market areas and customers to be served, tacit understandings quite similar to those which would be achieved by overt agreement are apt to arise. In the case of banks the tacit understandings . . . are abetted by public regulation and supervision which helps to assure that no individual bank will behave in a way which would have a strong competitive impact on others.

While there is no obvious solution to this problem, it may be that an atmosphere of public regulation designed to stimulate rather than to inhibit aggressive competition will have some beneficial effects.

III. Bank Portfolios and Services

1. Bank examination

Some stimulus to competition in banking can be achieved through revision of bank examination procedures. All insured commercial banks are examined by one of the Federal supervisory agencies. Traditionally the examiners have put great stress on safety and conservatism, and the highest compliment paid by an examiner was that management is "ultra-conservative." A former Comptroller of the Currency has pointed out: "Bank examination exercises a considerable influence on lending policies . . . through its insistence upon sound standards."[30]

The examiners criticize unsound or risky loans and investments but rarely criticize a bank for not vigorously competing for business or for

[28] The Comptroller of the Currency has ruled that "[a]greements, arrangements, or understandings among banks, through clearing houses or otherwise, concerning hours or days when such banks may be open for business are not permissible in any form." (*Comptroller Manual for National Banks*, 1964, Rulings § 7434.)

[29] "Competition, Confusion and Commercial Banking," p. 39.

[30] Statement of Preston Delano to Joint Committee on the Economic Report, *Monetary Policy and The Management of The Public Debt*, 82nd Cong., 2d Sess, p. 936.

not adequately serving local needs.[31] While there probably has been some change in this attitude in recent years, there is room for further change. If banks could be encouraged to seek more lending opportunities, competition would be increased in the loan markets. If, for example, all banks were to attempt to increase their loan/deposit ratio by, say, 3 percentage points, there would be a considerable increase in the supply of funds available for loans and thus considerable competitive pressure on loan rates. This does not mean that bankers should be encouraged to make unwise loans or that bankers should be encouraged to have a higher loan/deposit ratio than they consider prudent. The fact is, however, that there are some banks that restrain their lending activity not because they think further lending would be imprudent but because of a desire to avoid possible criticism by the bank examiners.[32]

The only detailed analysis of bank examination procedures and policies that has been published in recent years is the study of Donald Jacobs for the House Banking and Currency Committee.[33] Jacobs concluded that "[t]here is no doubt that bank examiners have an impact on bank loan and investment practices."[34] At times, moreover, this impact is an undesirable one. Jacobs places some of the blame for the curtailment of bank lending and the maintenance of large excess reserves during the 1930's on the bank examiners. He finds that the data on the 1930's:[35]

. . . suggest that the sharp decline in bank lending during that period was intensified by the activities of bank examiners . . . The maintenance of excess reserves that appeared during the 1930's can be explained, in part, as normal portfolio strategy by the banks. Their depleted capital position and the examiners' insistence that they were maintaining an overly high risk exposure in their loan portfolios dictated a reduction in risk, and this could be achieved primarily through shifts in their portfolios to assets classified as less risky.

[31] "Examiners are not especially interested in the justification of given loans from the standpoint of public welfare . . . but rather in the probabilities of their being repaid at maturity so that depositors will not be endangered by losses." Raymond Kent, *Money and Banking*, 4th ed (New York, 1961), p. 292. Note also the position of the FDIC on bank holdings of securities: "Banks are encouraged to limit their commitments to high grade bonds of short to medium term maturity." FDIC *Annual Report*, 1956, p. 5.

[32] As Comptroller Delano noted: "Officers and directors . . . know that by adhering to high standards, their bank will avoid criticism." *loc. cit.* An example of the possibility of affecting bank investment policy by examination procedures is the treatment by the regulatory authorities of paper losses on securities. Examiners must evaluate the capital position of a bank under examination. In calculating capital of the bank, however, paper losses on high-quality bonds are not deducted. If it were not for this policy, banks would be very reluctant to purchase long-term bonds.

[33] "The Impact of Examination Practices upon Commercial Bank Lending Policies," Subcommittee on Domestic Finance, Committee Banking and Currency, House of Representatives, 88th Cong., 2d Sess. 1964.

[34] *Ibid.*, p. 1.

[35] *Ibid.*, pp. 2, 33.

It is interesting to note that even at the present time Jacobs feels that "The bank examination process . . . tends to influence bank portfolio management toward maintaining a smaller ratio of loans to assets."[36]

The traditional role of the bank examiner has been that of protecting depositors. Perhaps we should give more stress to assuring that adequate credit will be made available to potential borrowers, and that examination standards themselves will not result in an undesirable reduction in the volume of bank assets. At least the examination procedure should not discourage the proper assumption of risk by commercial banks. The very low losses on loans incurred by banks in the post-war years (despite recent expression of concern about the "quality of credit") raise the question of whether the banks are assuming the risks they properly should.

2. Permissible loans and investments

Another means of increasing competition in the financial field is to lower some of the barriers that prevent or inhibit competition between banks and other financial institutions. The Comptroller of the Currency has in recent months issued certain rulings allowing national banks broader scope for their financial activities. National banks are now allowed to do direct lease financing. There is, of course, very little economic difference between direct leasing and making loans secured by equipment. Since there may be some advantages to users of the equipment to leasing rather than borrowing and purchasing equipment outright, this ruling increases the number of alternative suppliers available to the firm seeking to lease equipment.[37] That this increase in competition has been and will be effective is demonstrated by the strong opposition to this ruling by the leasing companies.[38]

Other recent rulings have liberalized the basis on which national banks can make loans secured by real estate. Again, this will increase competition in the mortgage lending field between commercial banks and savings and loan associations. As is to be expected, the latter have voiced considerable objection to such rulings.

National banks may now underwrite, in certain cases, securities which heretofore had been classified as revenue bonds and hence were not eligible for underwriting by national banks. This measure significantly increases competition in the municipal underwriting field. The increased

---

[36] *Ibid.*

[37] See Eugene F. Brigham, "The Impact of Commercial Bank Entry on Market Conditions in the Equipment Leasing Industry," *The National Banking Review*, September 1964.

[38] For an example of this opposition, see Alvin Zises, "Equipment Leasing By Banks: Problems and Solutions," *The Banker's Magazine*, Winter 1964. Mr. Zises is president of Bankers Leasing Corporation.

competition in municipal bond underwriting has had measurable effects on the prices of bonds declared eligible for underwriting by national banks. For example, following a ruling that bonds of various Georgia State Authorities could be underwritten and dealt in by national banks, there was an immediate increase in the market price of all such bonds. An issue of Georgia Highway Authority bonds which was selling at a yield of 3.30% on the Friday before the ruling was yielding 3.15% by the following Friday. The advantages of this increased competition to state and local governments, and hence to the general public, is clear despite the opposition of the investment banking industry.

The revenue bond underwriting case is an excellent example of the difficulties involved in stimulating competition through legislation. A bill introduced in Congress to do approximately the same thing as the Comptroller's ruling has run into strong opposition from the Investment Bankers Association and its passage is by no means certain.

The basic argument of the leasing companies, investment bankers and savings and loan associations in these matters is that they have developed techniques, and invested in the business involved, because of the limitations on commercial bank participation in the field. They argue that removal of the barriers on commercial banks is a change in the rules of the game and is unfair to them.

Their protests at new competition from an unexpected quarter are not unexpected and not entirely unjustified. In general, however, in a free economy no group should be able to stake a claim on any particular type of financing business and expect the government to respect that claim. Changes in the rules of the game are part of the game. The investment bankers have no claim to freedom from commercial bank competition in the municipal underwriting field, the leasing companies have no claim on sole possession of the leasing fields, and the savings and loan associations must be prepared to meet increased competition from commercial banks.[39]

Most of the regulatory actions discussed in this paper involve reducing restrictions on commercial bank operations. The question is frequently raised as to whether allowing banks to engage in "risky" activities (leasing, revenue bond underwriting, etc.) or to compete more freely on a price basis, may lead to serious danger of widespread bank failures. That is, if we substitute reliance on bankers' judgement and the free

---

[39] Of course, commercial bankers have often taken the other side of this argument in opposing extension of the powers of other institutions, mainly savings and loan associations. Certainly a beneficial effect on competition would result if savings and loans were allowed to make consumer instalment loans. There are complications here, however. Savings and loans have been given considerable tax benefits as part of a public policy to encourage home ownership. Even assuming that there is some logic to this policy, there would be no justification for continuing the special tax treatment of savings and loans if they became general purpose lenders.

market for regulation, will profit-maximizing behavior lead to greater risk-taking than is socially desirable?[40]

There is reason to believe that the traditional conservatism of most bankers would tend to restrain excessive risk-taking even in the absence of regulation. Alhadeff has pointed out that in "many institutions, regulatory restrictions merely reinforce actions which operating conventions would dictate in the absence of those regulations."[41]

Apart from traditional conservatism or adherence to cautious operating conventions, there are other restraints on the desire of bankers to take risks. Bank stockholders are not anxious to lose their investment even though depositors would share the loss. But the market provides a still more important restraint. Banks must attract deposits in order to earn profits and large depositors, who are *not* protected by deposit insurance, will evaluate the riskiness of banks before making a decision among alternatives. Part of the competition for large deposits involves competition in safety. A bank which goes too far in the direction of risky assets will tend to lose deposits, and thus purely in the interest of profit maximization a bank will find it desirable to avoid undue risk-taking. As long as this incentive to conservatism exists, it is unnecessary to require excessive conservatism through regulation.[42]

IV. Conclusions

Most of the measures discussed above involve freeing banks from regulations which restrain their activities. I have argued that many of these are unnecessary, and in many cases administrative decisions or changes in emphasis by various federal and state supervisory agencies can improve the level of competition in banking.

Actions taken by the banking regulatory authorities cannot, of

[40] It is important to note why this is a problem in banking but not in other industries. If a manufacturer takes too great a risk and fails, the loss is suffered, for the most part, by stockholders. When a bank fails, a large part of the loss is borne by depositors. Thus risk-taking bank stockholders reap all of the gain if the risk is successful, but share the loss with depositors if they are unsuccessful. Thus the incentive to excessive risk-taking by banks.

[41] David A. Alhadeff, "The Commission on Money and Credit's Research Studies," *Journal of Finance*, September 1964, p. 524.

[42] The strength of this incentive rests upon the importance to the bank of depositors whose accounts are not insured. If deposits were insured in full, as has frequently been proposed, this incentive would be eliminated. This effect should be considered in evaluating such proposals.

The strength of this effect also depends upon the ability of large depositors to obtain adequate information to evaluate the financial position of banks. This is made difficult by the failure of many banks to publish sufficient relevant data. Data on valuation reserves is the most significant such omission. The regulatory agencies should require disclosure of valuation reserves, in connection with the regular publication of the report of condition, as was done by the Comptroller in September 1963 but not subsequently.

course, make banking a perfectly competitive industry. There is certainly a need for legislation to improve competition in the financial field.[43] Nevertheless, it is important to realize that even within our present statutory framework it is possible to make some improvements in banking competition through administrative action by the regulatory authorities.

[43] Legislation is necessary, for example, to obtain the full competitive benefits of branch banking. Also, since many of the restrictions on bank operations are part of the law, legislation is required to eliminate them.

3

Banking structure and competition

*Howard D. Crosse**

This session of the American Finance Association meetings has been concerned with various aspects of the problems of banking structure and competition. Ted Flechsig's paper, I think, has been especially important because his conclusions tend to shatter a widely believed myth. He has shown that rates on business loans are not significantly related to concentration, but rather to size of loan, to geographical region and to loan characteristics (difficult as the last factor is to analyze).

The Justice Department *and* the Supreme Court should carefully study his conclusions. You will see from my subsequent comments that I do not disagree with them.

George Benston has used the functional cost data of the Federal Reserve Bank of Boston to compare the operating costs of branch banking with those of unit banks with respect (as nearly as possible) to the same services. He finds that the costs of providing services through more than a few branches tend to exceed whatever economies of scale may be inherent in a larger banking organization, principally because of higher occupancy expense. Unfortunately his data do not clearly distinguish between branches acquired by merger and those established *de novo*. With respect to the latter, the building obviously precedes the business—occasionally for considerable periods of time.

Donald Jacobs has discussed the interrelationship between branch restrictions and other regulations of banking with particular reference to restrictions on entry, interest rate regulation, and limitations on lending. His basic premise seems to be that structural characteristics are meaningfully related to performance characteristics. As I shall explain later, I find these relationships rather tenuous. In experience I find too

Reprinted with permission from *The Journal of Finance*, Vol. XX, No. 2 (May, 1965), pp. 349-357.

* Federal Reserve Bank of New York and New York University.

many exceptions to prove such a rule. More importantly, I find it entirely frustrating to discuss either concentration or competition on a statewide basis. I agree with Shull and Horvitz—who in "Branch Banking and the Structure of Competition"[1] found that,

In non-metropolitan areas, on average there are no fewer competitors in branch banking states than in unit banking states in the most relevant geographic banking markets, i.e. the *local market!* [Emphasis supplied.]

The small business man for whom bleeds the heart of both the economist and the regulatory agency is interested first (and perhaps last and all the time) in the availability of credit. As we have been recently reading in the press, he will get it from a loan shark if he cannot get it elsewhere. He is certainly more interested in the alternatives available in his own community, and in their understanding of his credit problems, than he is in the number of banks in the state. Three branches of different statewide banks provide far greater competition than a single unit bank on Main Street in any town!

But, I digress.

Rather than take issue with specific assumptions in any of the papers you have heard, I think it will serve our purpose better if I attempt to present, in broad brush strokes, some observations based on my supervisory experience. As Bob Holland, of the Board's staff has put it:[2] "There is no substitute for the guidance provided by intimate supervisory knowledge of many individual market situations." I agree with him also that "an invaluable complement to such knowledge, however, can be provided by objective research into the various facets of banking market performance under regulated conditions.

As a bank supervisor I come before you in the guise of a mystic: one to whom the Truth has been revealed—but who cannot prove it with statistics. I hope, in time, you will be able to demonstrate its validity.

I am reminded of an occasion many years ago when I rode from the Board building in Washington with a group of Reserve Bank economists who had apparently been discussing all day why excess reserves accumulate in country banks. They still could not understand this uneconomic behavior. The profit-minded economic man will seek to invest excess reserves! I listened for a while and finally asked, "Have any of you ever examined small country banks?" They hadn't, obviously, and I said, "Well, if you had you would understand perfectly why not only excess reserves, but back numbers of banking periodicals, and even instructions from the supervisor, pile up in country banks. You should see the desks of country bankers!"

---

[1] *The National Banking Review*, Vol I, No. 3 (March, 1964), pp. 340-1.
[2] "Research into Banking Structure and Competition," Federal Reserve *Bulletin*, November, 1964, p. 1384.

One of our large branch banks recently acquired a small country bank through merger. They found the vault so cluttered with back numbers of the *Herald Tribune* and empty cigar boxes (sometimes useful repositories of cash) that there was no room for needed additional safe deposit boxes. How can you measure economies of scale in such circumstances?

I could regale you with many such stories. They underlie the mystic truths of experience I shall try to propound. But first let us establish some sort of logical framework for the many cross-currents that complicate the problems of banking structure and competition.

As a matter of public policy we want the best banking structure we can have. The big question is "The best for whom?" If it were only the bank stockholder, we could leave banking structure to market forces and the Department of Justice. But we are talking about money in which everybody has a vital interest. At some risk of oversimplification we can examine separately the interests of the depositor, the borrower, the stockholder and what I call for lack of a better term, the general public, my own particular boss.

The depositor is interested in the safety of his particular deposit; he is interested in compensation for the use of his money either in the form of interest or services. He is interested in the efficiency of his bank as reflected in the accuracy of the posting of entries to his account. And finally he is interested in an intangible quality which I shall call "recognition." He resents having a bank teller ask him whether he has an account in the bank. He wants to be known to *his* bank. Hodgman has shown that banks value "relationship."[3] So do customers.

The borrower from a bank (who of course may also be a depositor) wants availability of credit first, understanding of his business or credit needs second, and a competitive rate, somewhere down the line. He is less interested in the absolute rate than in knowing that his bank is not charging him any more than another bank would.

The stockholder, or management as his proxy, wants maximum profitability. If he is wise he is looking to maximize profits over time. He will recognize that the long-range success of the bank is intimately interwoven with the growth and prosperity of the community it serves; that maximum success is not possible, in short, without satisfying both depositors and borrowing customers.

The public interest is not much different, but is broader in scope. It is concerned less with individual banks than with the banking system. Deposit insurance and bank examination for example, are evidence of public concern with deposit safety.

The public concern is with an efficient payments system rather than

[3] Donald R. Hodgman, *Commercial Bank Loan and Investment Policies*, Bureau of Economic and Business Research, University of Illinois, Champaign, 1963.

the correct posting of an individual's pay check. The public can ignore or shore up an individual bank failure but regulates banks closely to prevent widespread failures. And the public is vitally concerned with competition: it wants enough to insure generally good service at reasonable prices to the broad aggregate of individual borrowers and depositors —but not so much as to threaten bank failures.

I am sure that we all recognize that this catalogue of objectives contains numerous contradictions. Nationwide branch banking, as in Canada, has proved to be more failure-resistant than our widely diffused system. But is it sufficiently competitive to assure adequate credit at reasonable prices? There is clearly much that we need to know before we can definitely answer such questions. That which we need to know is both the subject of your research and of our supervisory concern. It is important, as a minimum, that we do not start such research with a bundle of misconceptions or biases that can only confuse our thinking or lead us down blind alleys.

There can be little question but there are great pressures in the economy for a more concentrated banking structure. Without regulatory controls there would be a great many more mergers and a great many more new branches established. This trend represents the judgment of bank management representing the long-range interests of the stockholder. These are the views of management both in the acquiring banks and those that are acquired. It takes two to tango! It is clear that bankers believe sincerely that there are efficiencies of scale, if not economies. And I think they are right.

The revealed truth, to which I testify, is that these pressures are directly related to economic growth and to the changing needs for banking services which economic growth brings about. No two situations are ever exactly alike, but let us take as one typical example a bank in a suburban community such as the one in which I myself live. Twenty years ago the community's simple banking needs were more or less well-served by a small local bank operated in a very unimaginative fashion. Loans from this bank were hard to obtain but there was little demand for credit in the community. The bank was eminently safe. It was convenient, and everyone in the community was personally known to the tellers and officers. Most of the customers had lived in the community for years; had in fact grown up there, and their parents and often their grandparents had been equally well-known. This is a clear advantage if your reputation in the community is a good one.

Then came economic growth. During the past twenty years the population of the community more than doubled. Hundreds of new homes were built; most of them financed outside of the community. The town is now to a much greater extent the home of transient executives. New businesses have come into being to service the needs of the increased population. New credit demands came along with them. Management of the local bank was unable to accommodate itself to these changing conditions. It didn't want to do business with strangers. It knew nothing about consumer credit. It couldn't understand the financial statements of the new businesses. It had no expertise in lending except against stock market collateral. It sat by frustrated and helpless watching a great deal of local business go to banks in neighboring towns.

At the same time the larger banks in the area eyed this growing community as a lucrative potential source of additional profitable business. With their well-developed consumer credit and mortgage departments, with their eager young commercial lending officers learning all about term loans and accounts receivable financing, they viewed themselves, and I think correctly, as much better able to serve the community's credit needs and able too, because of higher loan/deposit ratios to pay higher rates for savings deposits. To make a well-known story short, ten years ago the small banker sold out to the highest bidder—the largest bank in the county. He could not cope with the problems of growth and change.

The story is not much different in the rural areas where larger farms require larger credits and more lending expertise than small local banks are able to supply. And let me stress the expertise, for it is of even greater importance than lending limits. Any small bank can lend a customer whom it has known for years $1,000 to buy a new car. But this is a far cry from financing the retail paper of a local Ford dealer in a rapidly growing community, where half the borrowers are strangers, and especially if floor planning of inventory is also involved. Financing consumer credit in volume, if it is to be done safely, requires specialized skills and experience which small banks simply do not have. Nor do they have volume enough to justify developing these skills even if they could.

So, where permitted by law, we have more mergers, more branches, and less banking units. What are the results of this trend for the various public interests we have enumerated? George Benston has indicated some increase in the cost of doing business, and bankers generally recognize that theirs is becoming more and more a high volume and low profit margin business. Ted Flechsig has seen no important effect on lending rates as the result of concentration, and I agree with his findings. Don Jacobs has found a tendency for branch banks to concentrate on consumer lending, but I think that this is more a function of the markets branches serve than a question of structure. I cannot agree with his suspicion that large banks use the convenience of branches as a substitute for rate. In the Second Federal Reserve District, at least, the larger branch banks generally pay the highest rates on time and savings deposits. We must all agree, I think, that large branch banks, serving diversified areas, are safer and, because of their size and strength, can afford to take greater risks in individual credit situations. They can, and do make credit available where small unit banks do not.

More specifically, a number of things happen when a relatively small bank is merged into a large bank; happenings which, in fact, tend to confuse the statistics which have served as a basis for such studies as George Benston's and many others. The large bank immediately assumes what I have called the "prospective costs" which lead to bank mergers.[4] The first thing is a complete refurbishing of building and equipment at considerable expense. Then the employees of the small bank are brought into the salary program and pension plan of the larger bank which appreciably raises salary costs. Under most merger agreements, former management is retained, at least for a while, but the need for succession is met by bringing in an additional officer or two at the large bank's salary scale. The acquiring bank also usually pays the competitive rate on time and savings deposits which in many cases is more than the absorbed bank was paying. Thus the new branch starts off immediately with higher costs than the former unit bank. But it is *not* the same bank, either in appearance or in capacity for rendering banking services.

To recoup what it can of these additional costs, the large bank centralizes a number of functions. The investment account and money position are invariably transferred to the head office. The mortgage account and consumer loans are often centralized where they can be more efficiently handled in volume. Bookkeeping, at least for demand deposits, is consolidated. In these procedures I think there are evident economies of scale. They will become more objectively measurable when increased participation of larger banks in the functional cost analysis program permits comparison of the processing costs of varying volumes of essentially similar items such as mortgages, consumer loans, et cetera.

The large bank also tends to impose higher (and I think more realistic) service charges on deposit accounts. One product of the functional cost studies used by George Benston was the clear demonstration that small banks generally recover a relatively smaller portion of their processing costs through service charges. The depositors' gain on this score is, in my opinion, at the cost of the better facilities and better management which, as I have pointed out above, the larger bank immediately sets out to supply.

Our experience also bears out the conclusion of several studies[5] that branch banks tend to be more aggressive lenders. In nearly every case the former unit bank increases the outstanding total of its loans, often dramatically. Again this increase is often difficult to measure statistically

[4] Howard D. Crosse, *Management Policies for Commercial Banks,* Prentice-Hall, Inc. (Englewood Cliffs, N.J.), 1962.

[5] Irving Schweiger and John S. McGee, "Chicago Banking," *The Journal of Business* of the University of Chicago, July 1961.

because of the transfer of mortgage and consumer credit loans to the head office controls. However, in one quite typical case where one of three relatively small banks in a community was acquired through merger, it increased its loans by 170 per cent in the following five years, while the loans of the remaining unit banks increased only 63 and 64 per cent respectively.

At the same time the larger bank brings not only greater expertness to its customer relations but frequently provides new services (investment advisory services for example) which were not previously available and which do not show up on the branch balance sheet.

In short, comparison of unit banks with branch banks (particularly the 8,000 or so unit banks with total resources of less than $5 million), when such comparisons do not take into account the upgrading of product, have the effect of comparing a Model A Ford with a Galaxie without reference to horsepower or chrome trim.

Not everything, of course, is pure gain. What may be lost is some measure of that personal relationship which I have called "recognition," a psychic benefit of considerable importance to many bank customers as well as some bank regulators and members of Congress. The large bank, despite its stepped-up public relations "program," tends to be more impersonal, although many large banks, recognizing this danger, have taken specific steps to alleviate it. I read recently of a large branch organization which had created specialized departments for both "senior citizens" and young executives. The Franklin National Bank is planning an exclusive New York office which will provide highly personalized services in three languages to those who can afford it. Furthermore, I have never been able to determine to what extent the tendency to impersonalization is a result of branch banking or the natural concomitant of the suburbanization and economic growth which brought about the changes in banking structure. I'll leave that one to the sociologists.

One must admit too, that the results of these structural changes are themselves not uniform. The most important factor in the way an individual bank performs, whether it is a small bank or a large branch organization, is, and always will be, its management. Differences between individual banks of similar structure are often far greater than the differences between small banks and large, or branches and unit banks in general.

There are, for example, two large branch banks in the Second District with similar deposit totals and almost exactly the same number of branches. One bank formerly employed over 600 more people than the other. Despite a somewhat lower salary scale, its operations were clearly more costly and less efficient, with all the implications that that can have for staff morale and quality of services rendered. New management in this less efficient bank, addressing itself specifically to this problem, was able to reduce its staff by 125 people in less than a year. At which point in time is its performance typical of "large branch banks" of a certain size?

On the other hand, one of the most profitable banks by far in the Second Reserve District is a $16 million unit bank which last year had net current earnings of 3.1 per cent of assets (three times the average) and salary expenses of 11 per cent of gross income (half the average). These are the almost unbelievable results of unusually competent management regardless of size or structure. Somehow, as a supervisor, I have always been more interested in what well-managed banks *can* do than in what average banks actually accomplish.

Management also makes the difference with respect to the way small banks meet the challenge of a developing economy. The story of frustration and merger I related earlier may be typical but is far from inevitable. I am thinking of a bank in rapidly expanding Suffolk County, New York, which in 1955 (less than 10 years ago) had total resources of less than $3 million. Today, without benefit of any merger, it operates six branches, all established *de novo*, and has resources of $41 million. In this case, dynamic and effective management met the challenge of changing times.

Our supervisory knowledge of just how much difference the quality of management can make tends to make us suspect of generalizations based on statistics which do not take the quality of management into account. It is my deep conviction that, for all the various groups that are looking to our banking system for both economic and psychic benefits, management is a far more important factor than either size or structure. The real function of competition in banking, it seems to me, is to exert pressure for improved management. We see this pressure frequently being exerted by well-managed branches of large banks on the small bank which does not have the management capacity to adjust to economic changes. We have also seen it exerted by the small gadfly challenging the established giants with new ideas or highly developed specialties. To keep this challenge ever fresh, I am sure you will agree, we must preserve the "right of entry."

Academicians tend to think of entry almost exclusively in terms of new banks. They have often accused the supervisor of barring the way for many prospective entrants.[6] Donald Jacobs' presentation seemed to talk of entry restrictions as applying only to new banks. If we define entry, however, as the creation of a new competitive force in a local banking market, we must concede that the establishment of a branch, either *de novo* or by merger, does intensify competition. In the community I mentioned earlier, for example, where one of three small local banks

[6] Cf. David A. Alhadeff, "A Reconsideration of Restrictions on Bank Entry," *Quarterly Journal of Economics*, 76 (May 1962), pp. 246-63.

was acquired by a county-wide branch organization, the greater management ability of the larger and more aggressive bank immediately put pressures on the other local banks to improve their service to the community. One brought in new management—the other sought, itself, to merge with a larger bank. Entry by branching, in fact, is much more effective than entry through the formation of another bank because it brings into the community immediately the well-developed management techniques and capabilities of an established organization.

The real bars to "entry" are the bars to branching, including those laws in states which permit branching but prohibit the establishment of *de novo* branches in communities already served by other banks; the so-called "home office protection" laws. In New Jersey it is so bad that, except in a town served by its head office, a bank may not establish a branch in any municipality already served by another branch, even one of its own! Laws which limit branching create an obvious bias in favor of new banks as the only available means of entry.

As a bank supervisor I am somewhat sensitive on the subject of new banks. I have never seen a charter denied where a proposed bank, by any stretch of the imagination, could have become a viable competitive force. I have seen many granted to banks which have never become viable. Needs and convenience, the criteria which Alhadeff found to be too strictly applied, are used by the chartering authorities as being broadly synonymous with "chances for success." The supervisory statement denying a charter may read in terms of needs and convenience, but more often than not, what will have been found lacking is management. No bank supervisor who wants to avoid suits for defamation of character can afford to announce publicly that he is denying a charter because he questions the business ethics of the organizers, or even express his doubts as to their credit-worthiness. He is going to find, publicly, a lack of need!

Alhadeff assumed that bank organizers know what they are doing. As one who has met with numerous would-be organizers over the years, I can testify that this just is not so. Most often they have little or no concept of the problems of running a bank successfully. I remember one attorney who discussed with me the organization of a bank to serve the peculiar credit needs of small diamond mrchants. He was going to put the bank on the second floor of an obscure building in the knowledge that these borrowers would have no trouble finding it. I asked, "What about the depositors? Where are you going to get the money to lend?" He hadn't thought of that!

While this is an extreme example, let me assure you that few potentially viable banks have been denied charters. The rock on which most unsuccessful applicants founder is lack of responsible management (including directors). Many that were granted charters have had the same problem, unfortunately, and have had to be absorbed to bail them out of the difficulties poor management got them into.

On the other hand, when proposed new banks are sponsored by financially responsible and public-spirited organizers who engage competent operating management, the application is warmly welcomed by the supervisor.

To summarize, then, it has been my observation that banking structure and competition need to be studied more closely in terms of effective markets. For all but the larger corporations which have wide choices of alternatives, these are local markets. In all markets, it seems to me, the most dynamic competitive force is that of imaginative and effective (albeit prudent) management. Fortunately that kind of management is not the exclusive prerogative of any particular form of banking organization. Well-managed small banks are often more effective competitors in local markets than the branches of the largest banks.

While the right of entry of well-managed new banks should be zealously preserved, relaxation of branching restrictions will greatly intensify competition in many local markets, affording the user of bank services, both depositor and borrower, with a wider choice of expert service. I suspect that the banking public will do an increasing amount of its "shopping" in the "department stores" of banking as Don Jacobs calls them, but that there will always be a place for the well-run specialty shop and the delicatessen.

4

Branch banking and economies of scale

*George J. Benston**

I. Introduction

Which organizational form, unit or branch, for the banking industry best serves the public welfare? This question has prompted much of the recent research on the organization of the banking industry. This paper focuses on one unresolved aspect of this larger question; namely, which form is most efficient with respect to private costs and benefits. The empirical findings reported here hopefully will complement the recent, excellent research done on the relative ability and desire of branch and unit banks to serve local communities.[1]

The controversy between unit and branch banking supporters would be simplified if entry into the banking industry was not restricted; then we could say, "let the best bank win." However, even with free entry and no limitations on the form of organization of banks, it still would not be clear whether the successful banks were those that operated most efficiently or those that were able to maintain oligopolistic market arrangements. Therefore, it is important to determine whether the branch or unit form of bank organization is inherently more efficient.

Reprinted with permission from *The Journal of Finance*, Vol. XX, No. 2 (May, 1965), pp. 312-331.

* University of Chicago.
The help in preparing this paper given by Jacob Michaelsen is gratefully acknowledged.
[1] A few examples are New York State Banking Department, *Branch Banking, Bank Mergers, and the Public Interest* (New York, 1964), Bernard Shull and Paul M. Horvitz, "Branch Banking and the Structure of Competition," *National Banking Review* (I, March, 1964), pp. 301-41, and Clifton H. Kreps, Jr., "Local Banking Competition in Three Metropolitan Areas," Federal Reserve Bank of Richmond (Richmond, 1964). A more complete bibliography is given by Robert C. Holland in "Research into Banking Structure and Competition," School Reserve Bulletin, 50 (November, 1964), pp. 1383-99.

This paper focuses on the costs of banking operations. Excluded from consideration are differences between branch and unit banks that might arise from differences in fun acquiring and fund using opportunities, capital requirements, and ability to get approval from the regulatory agencies to establish new offices. Rather, my inquiry is limited to the costs of processing deposits, loans and securities, of administration, business promotion and occupancy—in short, the costs of operating banks.

Differences in operating costs between branch and unit banks may arise from two sources. First, branch banks, *per se*, may be more or less costly to operate than unit banks of the same size. Second, branch banks may be able to grow larger than unit banks and take advantage of economies that may come from large scale operations.

The claims and counter-claims about relative operating efficiencies usually have been supported by descriptive reasoning. For example, opponents of branch banking claim that branch banks have higher operating costs than unit banks that possess the same output because it is costly to coordinate the operations of more than one banking office. Branch banking proponents counter with the assertion that branch banks tend to employ more "progressive" branch managers who operate their branches more efficiently than the department managers of unit banks operate their departments. Economies of large scale operations are claimed for branch banks because they usually are larger than unit banks. That economies of scale do exist has been generally assumed rather than demonstrated.

My study is directed towards providing empirical evidence (1) on the operations costs or cost savings associated with branch banking, *per se*, (2) on the economies or diseconomies of scale excluding consideration of branch banking and (3) on the joint effects of (1) and (2). Thus answers are provided to the following questions:

1. Is a unit bank of a given size more efficient than a branch bank of the same size, *ceteris paribus*, and, if so, how much are these costs and in which specific banking services are they found?

2. If a bank should increase its demand deposits, instalment loans, or other banking service by, say, ten per cent, by what percentage will its costs increase, irrespective of its being a unit or branch bank?

3. If branch banks, *per se*, are more expensive operate than unit banks, but if there are economies of scale, will merging several unit banks into one branch bank result in lower or higher operating costs, and in which banking services will these net costs or cost savings be found?

The data and method of analysis used for this study are described in Section II. The findings derived from these data are presented in detail in Section III and summarized in Section IV. These findings are compared with those of other published studies in Section V. A brief conclusion follows.

II. Data and Analyses Used[2]

I analysed the operating cost and output data from sample of 83, 82 and 80 New England member banks for the years 1959, 1960 and 1961.[3] Because the banks ranged in size from $3.5 to $55.0 million in total assets, these samples are not fully representative of the population of United States banks although over half of the number of commercial banks in the United States are within this range.[4] Further, the largest branch bank in the sample operated twelve branches, far short of such giant branching systems as the Bank of America or Chase-Manhattan. In spite of these limitations, this study can serve as a useful supplement to the broader based data noted below.[5]

The data upon which the study is based were gathered by the Federal Reserve Bank of Boston. The Bank has conducted a cost analysis service for member banks in the First Federal Reserve District since 1957. Staff from the participating banks attend a seminar in which they are given detailed instructions on filling in the cost analysis forms. They allocate direct costs to the banking services of demand deposits, time deposits, mortgage loans, instalment loans, business loans and securities. Many costs are easy to allocate: savings tellers work only on time deposits and specific loan forms are related to the loans made. However, some costs, such as the salary of an officer in a small bank who makes all types of loans, had to be allocated. These allocations of salaries are based on time sheets. Other costs are allocated by means of specific analyses. Most of the banks included in the samples had several years of experience in filling in the forms, and the data they reported were carefully checked by the staff of the Federal Reserve Bank of Boston.

The costs of banking operations were analysed as a function of output, product mix, branch and unit banking, factor prices, mergers, and other variables that affect costs.

Output is defined as the average number of deposit accounts or loans outstanding during the year. An average of the number outstanding at each month end was computed to reduce the effect of randomness and to approximate more closely the flow of work processed rather than

---

[2] A much more detailed description of the data and methods of analysis used is presented in another paper, "Marginal Costs and Economics of Scale in Banking Operations," *National Banking Review*, June, 1965.

[3] 50 of the banks are included in all three samples.

[4] In 1960, over 52 per cent of the population of banks were in this asset range.

[5] A comparison presented in Section V indicates that the data used in the present study are consistent with data from all member banks.

the stock of work on hand at a particular time. This variable, instead of the dollar volume of loans and securities, was used because the operations work of banks, and hence costs, is closely related to the number of deposit accounts and loans they process. Had output been defined as the dollar volume of loans and securities, a finding of lower costs per dollar that results from a bank's having processed accounts and loans with larger outstanding balances might have been mistaken for operating efficiency.

The effect of product mix on operations costs was controlled by analysing relatively homogeneous banking services individually. Six banking services distinguished: demand deposits, time deposits, mortgage loans, instalment loans, business loans, and securities. Intercorrelations among these services were controlled and accounted for by three methods: (1) indirect costs, which affect all of the banking services, were not included with direct costs but were analysed separately, (2) "total assets" or a similar variable was included in each of the banking service regressions to estimate the effect of over-all bank size on individual services, and (3) variables that specified outputs of banking services that are related to the one analysed were included in the regressions where specific interrelations of possible joint cost situations were thought to exist.[6] Indirect costs were separated into three categories: administration, business development, and occupancy expenses. These were analysed individually.

Analysis of each banking service and type of indirect cost separately enables a determination of the specific banking function with which economies of scale and/or branch banking costs are associated. This identification should be helpful for policy decisions.

Table 1. Percentage Distribution of Unit and Branch Banks

| Year | Unit Banks | Branch Total | Number of Branches | | | | |
			One	Two	Three	Four	Five to Twelve
1959	55%	45%	17%	17%	7%	4%	0%
1960	45	55	17	15	12	4	7
1961	44	56	18	14	11	5	8

Approximately half of the sampled banks are branch banks, as Table 1 shows. The effect of branch banking on costs was estimated by including one of three possible variable forms in the regressions: (1) the number of banking offices (NO); (2) a dummy variable where $1 =$

---

[6] For example, "total time deposits" was included in the demand deposit regressions. However, it was of no significance.

branch bank and $0 =$ unit bank (B_o); and (3) a dummy variable matrix where:

$B_1 = 1$ for banks with one branch, 0 for other banks,
$B_2 = 1$ for banks with two branches, 0 for other banks,
$B_3 = 1$ for banks with three branches, 0 for other banks,
$B_4 = 1$ for banks with four branches, 0 for other banks,
$B_5 = 1$ for banks with five or more branches, 0 for other banks.

The form used was the one that caused the greatest reduction in the adjusted standard error of estimate.

The dummy variable matrix, which in most instances fits the data best, has several advantages over the other forms. This form requires the least specification of the functional relationship between branch banking and costs. By contrast, the branch-unit variable (B_o) used in the Horvitz and Schweiger-McGee studies noted below, and the number of offices variable (NO) assume a linear or dichotomous relationship. The dummy variable matrix also provides data on the consistency of the relationship between costs and branching. For example, a finding of significant coefficients only for the four-branch (B_4) but not for the other dummy variables would lead one to suspect the validity of conclusions drawn from the data.[7] Finally, the additional costs of operating different sized branching systems can be computed readily from the coefficients of the dummy variables.

Other determinants of operations costs, such as the average size of deposit and loan balances outstanding, factor prices, the rate of change and variability of output, mergers, the number of transit items, checks and deposits processed per demand deposit amount, etc, were accounted for by inclusion of additional independent variables in the regressions.

The variables were transformed to common logarithms for several reasons. First, this procedure resulted in approximate homoskedasticity among the residuals from the regressions.[8] Second, *a priori* reasoning suggested a multiplicative rather than an additive relationship among the variables. This is especially important for the branch banking variable, because any additional costs should be a function of the size of banks, rather than a constant amount (as was assumed by the additive functional relationhip used in the Schweiger-McGee study described below). Third, when the squares of the logarithms of the number of deposit accounts or loans were included as independent variables, the equation was

---

[7] Such was the case for the mortgage loan and time deposits data.
[8] Constants had to be added to direct costs and the number of accounts on loans for the time deposit and mortgage loans data before logarithms were taken. Otherwise, the logarithmic data would have been heteroskedastic.

capable of estimating any theoretically recognized cost curve. In this manner, the linearity assumption, for which cost studies often are criticized, was avoided.

III. The Findings for Individual Banking Services and Types of Indirect Expenses

The results of the analyses of the demand deposit, instalment loans, time deposits, mortgage loans, business loans and securities banking services and the indirect expenses of administration, business promotion and occupancy are given in this section. Substantial additional costs of branch banking were found for demand deposit, instalment loan and occupancy expenses, and small additional costs for indirect administration expenses.

Two types of tables are presented.[9] One (such as Table 2 below) shows the additional direct operations costs of the banking services of branch banks with various numbers of branches over unit banks, where all other factors (such as the level of output) are accounted for. The percentage increase in cost and the dollar amount computed at the geometric means of the output and other variables are given. These tables provide answers to the first question posed above: Is a unit bank more efficient than a branch bank of the same size, *ceterus paribus*, and if so, how much are these costs and in which specific banking services are they found? The additional costs of a four-branch bank over a three-branch bank, for example, also can be computed from these tables by simple subtraction.

The second table (such as Table 3 below) combines the effects of cost savings due to economies of scale with the additional costs of branch banking to answer the question: Will merging several unit banks into one branch bank result in lower or higher operating costs, and in which banking services will these net costs or cost savings be found? This table also shows the cost savings that are derived from economies of scale and the additional branch banking costs that are expected at the greater level of operations that a newly merged branch bank might experience. These estimates are given in terms of percentages of direct costs. Thus, for example, one can observe in Table 3 that a consolidation of five unit banks into a branch bank with four branches is estimated to result in additional direct demand deposit costs of 9.7 per cent from the 1960 sample. This percentage increase is the difference between the additional

---

[9] The variables from which these tables were computed are those for which the regression coefficients computed were greater than the standard errors of the coefficients. This "significance" rule is biased against the hypothesis that branch banks are as efficient as unit banks, as compared with the usual "5 per cent" significance test.

costs of branch banking that would be incurred at the new scale of operations of 24.1 per cent (28.2 per cent from Table 2 times 85.6, the elasticity of costs with respect to output at the new level of output) and the cost savings due to the increased scale of operations of 14.4 per cent.[10]

Demand deposit service

Demand deposit operations expenses average 35 per cent of the total operating expenses of the banks sampled. These expenses (in common logarithms) were analyzed as a function of the following independent variables (all of which are in common logarithms):

N_d = Average number of demand deposit accounts outstanding.

A_r = Average balance of regular checking accounts only.

SC_r = Service charge rate on regular checking accounts only.

WIN = Weighted activity items—checks, deposits, and transit items—per account.

RN_d = Ratio of the number of regular to the total number of accounts, in percentages.

W = Relative wages per employee in each bank's county.

$B_1, B_2,$
B_3, B_4, B_5 = Matrix of branch dummy variables described above, where $B_1 = 1$ for a bank with 1 branch and 0 for banks with other than one branch, etc.

The squares of the number of accounts (N_a), average balance of accounts (A_r) and weighted activity items per account (WIN) variables were included in the regression along with the non-squared forms, but they were subsequently omitted because they were not significant or were collinear with the unsquared terms.[11]

The one-branch variable (B_1) regression coefficient was smaller than the standard error of its coefficient and thus is not considered to be significant. The additional cost over unit banks of performing the same

[10] These calculations also can be shown by considering the following relationships. Let C_i = the operations costs of unit bank i. Then $\sum_i^n C = S =$ the sum of the costs of the unit banks that merged to form a branch bank. The new branch's costs are subject to economies of scale by the percentage E, and thus are equal to S·E, but also are higher due to the additional costs of branch banking by the percentage A. Thus, the branch bank's additional costs are equal to S(E·A) and its costs savings due to economies of scale are S(1 − E). E·A is the percentage increase due to branch banking and 1 − E the percentage decrease due to economies of scale.

[11] R^2's of the regressions are .96 for 1960 and .95 for 1961. A more meaningful indicator of "goodness of fit" is the percentage that the standard error of estimate is of the geometric mean of the dependent variable, in anti-logarithms. The percentages, hereafter called "standard error of estimate percentages," are 15 for 1950 and 17 for 1961.

volume of operations with two, three or four, etc., branches was computed from the regression coefficients of the branch banking dummy variables, all of which were at least two and one-half times the size of their standard errors. These are summarized in Table 2.

Table 2. Demand Deposit Service, Additional Direct Operations Cost of Branch Banking Over Unit Banking[a]

Number of Branches	Additional Cost Computed at Geometric Means		Percentage Increase in Cost	
	1960	1961	1960	1961
2 (B_2)	$22,400	$16,000	21.6	15.9
3 (B_3)	17,300	23,700	16.7	22.4
4 (B_4)	27,200	43,200	28.2	40.9
5+ (B_5)	39,100	38,200	37.7	36.2

[a] The regression run on the 1959 data is not useful because the data available are not comparable to those used in 1960 and 1961. Probably as a result, none of the forms of the "branches" variable are "significant" for the 1959 regression, though they are positive. (For this study, a "significant" coefficient is one that is at least as large as the standard error of the coefficient.) The one branch variable (B_1) is omitted because it is not "significant."

It is interesting to note that the increase in additional branch banking costs is less than proportional to the increase in the number of branches operated. Hence, it appears that additional branch banking costs *per banking office* decrease with the number of banking offices operated. Also the costs of banks that operated only one branch differed little from those of unit banks.

The elasticities (E) (and their standard errors) of direct operations costs with respect to output (N_a) estimated are .856 (.044) in 1960 and .809 (.052) in 1961. Table 3 summarizes the joint effect of the additional costs of branch banking presented in Table 2 and the elasticities.

Table 3. Demand Deposits, Additional Costs of Branch Banking (A) and Cost Savings Due to Scale of Operations, in Percentages

Number of Branches	Additional Cost of Branch Banking at New Scale of Operations ($A \times E$)		Cost Savings Due to Scale of Operations ($1 - E$)		Net Addition to Costs ($A \times E$) − ($1 - E$)	
	1960	1961	1960	1961	1960	1961
1 (B_1)	.0	.0	14.4	19.2	−14.4	−19.2
2 (B_2)	18.5	13.6	14.4	19.2	4.1	− 5.6
3 (B_3)	14.3	19.2	14.4	19.2	− 0.1	.0
4 (B_4)	24.1	35.0	14.4	19.2	9.7	15.8
5+ (B_5)	32.3	31.0	14.4	19.2	17.9	11.8

Thus the findings indicate that if two unit banks combine to form a branch bank with one branch, they would only experience cost savings due to economies of scale. It is not until five or more unit banks form a branch bank with four branches that net additional costs are experienced.

Minimization of cash and float is another important aspect of efficient demand deposit operations. To test for this, cash and float per $100 of deposits was regressed on the independent variables (except W) listed above. Not all of the branch dummy variables had regression coefficients that were larger than the standard errors of the coefficients in any one sample. The dummy variables that were "significant" were not the same ones among the samples nor were the signs consistently positive or negative. Hence, it is concluded that there is no measurable difference in efficient cash and float operations between unit and branch banks.

Instalment loans service

Instalment lending costs average 10 per cent of total operating costs, the highest percentage of the lending services. The following independent variables were used to analyze the direct annual operations cost of the instalment loans service (all variables in common logarithms):[12]

N_i = Average number of instalment loans outstanding.
A_i = Average balance of instalment loans.
Y_i = Earnings yield on loans.
W = Relative wages per employee in each bank's county.
NO = Number of banking offices (this variable was found to be more effective than the branch bank dummy variables).

The square of N_i and A_i were included in the regressions. N_i^2 alone superior to N_i or the combination of N_i and N_i^2. A_i^2 was not "significant."[13] Table 7 shows the additional cost of branch banking computed at the geometric means of the output and other variables and the percentage increase in cost due to branch banking computed from the coefficients of NO. The standard errors of these NO coefficients are less than half the magnitude of the coefficients.[14]

[12] The ratios of direct loans and indirect instalment loans to total instalment loans were tried as variables (floor plan loans were excluded to avoid over-identification). They were not meaningful, even when the samples were divided into unit and branch banks and run separately.

[13] R^2's of the regressions are .87 for 1959, .93 in 1960, and .91 in 1961. Standard error of estimate percentages are 34 for 1959, 25 for 1960 and 29 for 1961.

[14] It has been alleged that branch banks might have higher costs than unit banks because they accept riskier loans, which necessitate more investigation. Inclusion of Y_i as an independent variable should account for this difference, since riskier loans should bear greater gross yields than other loans. Since Y_i also could be a

The economies of scale found are not constant over the range of output but are the same among the samples. At the geometric mean of the number of loans (and ranges of plus and minus one standard deviation of the mean), the elasticity of direct operations cost with respect to output (N_i) is .881 (.757 to .948).

Table 4. Instalment Loans, Additional Direct Operations Cost of Branch Banking Over Unit Banking

Number of Branches	Additional Cost Computed at Geometric Means			Percentage Increase in Costs		
	1959	1960	1961	1959	1960	1961
1	$2,400	$2,680	$ 3,280	11.2%	9.1%	8.6%
2	3,930	4,350	5,330	18.3	14.6	14.0
3	5,070	5,610	6,850	23.6	19.1	18.0
4	5,940	6,600	8,010	27.6	22.4	21.0
8	—	9,160	11,070	—	31.2	29.1

Table 5. Instalment Loans, Additional Costs of Branch Banking (A) and Cost Savings Due to Scale of Operations, in Percentages

Number of Branches	Additional Cost of Branch Banking at New Scale of Operations (A × E)			Cost Savings Due to Scale of Operations (1 − E)[a]			Net Addition to Costs (A × E) − (1 − E)		
	1959	1960	1961	1959	1960	1961	1959	1960	1961
1	9.7	7.9	7.6	13.5	13.0	11.9	−3.8	−5.1	−4.3
2	16.2	12.9	12.7	11.3	11.8	9.3	4.9	1.1	3.4
3	21.3	17.0	16.7	9.6	10.9	7.5	11.7	6.1	9.2
4	25.3	20.2	19.7	8.4	10.0	6.1	16.9	10.2	13.6
8	—	28.6	28.4	—	8.4	2.4	—	20.2	26.0

[a] The elasticities tabled here were computed at the levels of outut (N_i) observed for each size of branch banking system.

Tables 4 and 5 indicate that groupings of small unit banks into branch banks would result in cost savings or small percentage increases in the cost of operations. However, the economies of scale are a decreasing function of output, so this advantage is limited to groupings of relatively small banks. Nevertheless, the *marginal* cost of branch banking

---

function of market factors, the samples were separated into unit banks and branch banks and the regressions recomputed. The coefficients measured for the sub-samples were the same as those computed for the whole sample. Any market differences, then, do not affect the cost estimates.

is a decreasing function of the number of branches operated. Thus, even if there were no economies of scale forthcoming, the *marginal* increase in the direct cost of operating an additional branch when eight branches are operated is only about two per cent.

Time deposits service

Interest paid on time deposits made up 85 per cent of the total direct expense of the time deposits service in the banks sampled. However, it was not included in the analysis because interest is not an operating cost subject to economies of scale but rather is primarily a function of market conditions. The remaining annual direct operations expenses are about 4 per cent of total operating expenses. The common logarithms of the time deposit operations expenses were analyzed as a function of the following variables (all of which are in common logarithms):

N_{tc} = Average number of time deposit accounts outstanding + 1000 (the constant was added before logarithms were taken to reduce heteroskedasticity).

A_t = Average balance of time deposit accounts.

RN_t = Ratio of savings accounts to savings accounts plus Christmas Club accounts.

W = Relative wages per employee in each bank's county.

B_1, B_2, B_3, B_4, B_5 = Matrix of branch dummy variables described above, where $B_1 = 1$ for a bank with 1 branch, 0 for banks with other than one branch, etc.

The squared terms of N_t and A_t and the ratio of time to total deposits also were included as independent variables. However, they were not "significant."[15]

The branch banking dummy variables are not consistently "significant" among the samples.[16] Those that are "significant" have coefficients approximating twice the size of the standard errors. Nevertheless, the additional costs of branch banking were computed and are included in Table 6.

Time deposit operations are also subject to economies of scale. The elasticity of direct operations cost with respect to output (N_t) increases

---

[15] R^2's of the regressions are .83 for 1959, .86 for 1960, and .86 for 1961. Standard error of estimate percentages are 31 for 1959, 33 for 1960, and 33 for 1961.

[16] When the excluded branch dummy variables are included in the regressions, their coefficients are smaller than the standard errors of the coefficients and are not consistent among the samples. Negative (though not "significant") coefficients were even found for B_1 and B_4 in 1960 and B_5 in 1961.

with output since constants were added to the dependent variable (direct cost) and to an independent variable (the number of accounts, N_t). At the geometric mean of output (N_{tc}), these elasticities (E) (and their ranges from mean less one standard deviation to mean plus one standard deviation) are .679 (.497 to .736) in 1959, .955 (.881 to .988) in 1960 and .878 (.797 to .912) in 1961.[17] Table 6 summarizes the joint effect on costs of additional branch costs and elasticities.

Table 6. Time Deposits, Additional Costs of Branch Banking (A) and Cost Savings Due to Scale of Operations, in Percentages

Number of Branches	Additional Cost of Branch Banking at New Scale of Operations (A × E)			Cost Savings Due to Scale of Operations (1 − E)a			Net Addition to Costs (A × E) − (1 − E)		
	1959	1960	1961	1959	1960	1961	1959	1960	1961
1 (B₁)	.0	.0	.0	32.1	4.5	12.2	−32.1	− 4.5	−12.2
2 (B₂)	35.7	.0	.0	31.0	4.5	12.2	4.7	− 4.5	−12.2
3 (B₃)	18.2	25.7	25.4	31.5	4.0	11.8	−13.3	21.7	13.6
4 (B₄)	.0	.0	41.6	32.1	4.5	11.3	−32.1	− 4.5	30.3
5+ (B₅)	—	.0	.0	—	4.5	12.2	—	− 4.5	−12.2

a Elasticities were computed at the level of output at the branches that experienced additional branch banking costs. Geometric mean elasticities were used for the other branch banks.

Mortgage loans

Mortgage lending expenses are only 2 per cent of total operating expenses. The mortgage loan data are similar to those for time deposits, in several ways: not all banks serviced mortgage loans; constants had to be added to the dependent and output variables to correct for heteroskedasticity, and the branch bank dummy variables behaved erratically. Direct operations cost plus $1000 was regressed on the average number of mortgage loans outstanding plus 100 (N_{mc}), the average balance of loans (A_m), relative wages (W), the ratio of mortgage loans to total loans and investments, and the branch bank dummy variables. However, only N_{mc} and A_m, in addition to some of the dummy variables, are "significant."[18] The dummy variables that have coefficients that are greater than the standard errors of the coefficients for all three samples are for the B_4 group, which includes no more than four banks. Therefore,

[17] The regression coefficients from which these elasticities were calculated are no less than twelve times as large as their standard error.

[18] R^2's of the regressions are .71 for 1959, .80 for 1960 and .81 for 1961. Standard error of estimate percentages are 33 for 1959, 37 for 1960, and 42 for 1961.

I concluded that there are no measurable additional costs of branch banking for the mortgage loans service.

Economies of operations costs with respect to output (N_m) were found. As was the situation with the time deposits data, the elasticities are an increasing function of the number of loans (N_m). At the geometric means of N_m, these elasticities (and the ranges from mean less one standard deviation to mean plus one standard deviation) are .851 (.698 to .920) for 1959, .811 (.767 to 1.064) for 1960 and .932 (.689 to 1.025) for 1961.[19]

Business loans service

None of the branch banking variables were useful in "explaining" the direct operations costs of the business loans service, since the standard errors of their coefficients were several times the size of the coefficients.[20] This finding is not surprising, since business lending most often is centralized in the main office. Therefore, the operations of a branch bank are not likely to be different from those of a unit bank that processes the same number and size of loans.

In addition, neither economies or diseconomies of scale were found. Thus, operations cost of the business loans service is neutral with respect to branch banking and scale of operations.

Securities

The direct costs of buying and selling securities average only 1 per cent of total operating expenses. Therefore, though economies of scale were measured, the effect of these on total operating expenses was less than a 0.5 per cent saving. Additionally, the coefficients of the branch banking dummy variables were not consistent among the samples either with respect to signs or "significance." Thus, the costs of the securities departments of the banks need not be considered further.

Indirect expenses

Indirect expenses average 43 per cent of total operating expenses in the banks sampled. In general, indirect expenses are related to the over-all activities of a bank. Total assets was used as a proxy variable for

---

[19] The regression coefficients from which the elasticities were computed are at least twelve times the size of the standard errors of the coefficients.

[20] The average number of loans, average balance of loans, interest yield earned, the ratio of business loans to total loans and investments, and relative wages are the "significant" variables. R^2's for the regressions are .79 for 1959, .83 for 1960, and .79 for 1961. Standard errors of estimate percentages are 38 for 1959, 36 for 1960, and 43 for 1961.

this over-all activity.[21] In addition, the following variables were included to account for cost differences due to differences in product mix:

D/TD = Ratio of demand deposits to total deposits, in percentages.
M/LS = Ratio of mortgage loans to total loans and securities, in percentages.[22]
I/LS = Ratio of instalment loans to total loans and securities, in percentages.[23]
B/LS = Ratio of business loans to total loans and securities, in percentages.[24,25]
S/LS = Ratio of securities to loans and securities, in percentages.[26]

All of the variables were transformed to common logarithms.

The output and product mix variables, their squares, and the branch banking variables were regressed on three categories of indirect expenses: administration expenses, business promotion expenses and occupancy expenses. Separation of indirect expenses into these groups allows a further delineation of the specific areas in which economies and additional branch banking costs may exist. Improved specification is achieved also since it is likely that differences in scale, product mix and branch banking have differing effects on each category of indirect expenses. Each of the indirect expense groups are discussed in turn below.

Administration expenses

Administration expenses comprise approximately 27 per cent of total operating expenses. The salaries and fringe benefits of executive officers and the board of directors make up about 65 per cent of this expense group. The balance includes general printing, office equipment rentals and depreciation, legal and other professional fees, examination and audit costs, etc.

In addition to the scale (TA) and the number of offices (NO) variables, D/TD, I/LS, S/LS and $(S/LS)^2$ were significant "in explaining" the costs.[27] However, the regression coefficients (and standard errors) of NO are .056 (.054) for 1959, .114 (.051) for 1960, and (.074)

---

[21] Total loans and securities could have been used, but the results would have been equivalent since it is correlated +.99 with total assets.

[22] All of the ratios of loans or securities to total loans and securities were not included in the same regression. B/LS usually was excluded.

[23] *Ibid.*

[24] *Ibid.*

[25] B/LS was not used in the same regression as D/TD since the two are highly correlated.

[26] See footnote 22.

[27] R^2's of the regressions are .88 for 1959, .91 for 1960, .83 for 1961. Standard error of estimate percentages are 30 for 1959, 24 for 1960 and 37 for 1964.

for 1961. Therefore, the additional costs computed and presented in Table 9 for 1959 and 1961 should be viewed as subject to considerable error. While the economies of scale (E) are slight, it is interesting to note that they are greatest for 1960, the only sample in which the coefficient of the NO variable was much greater than its standard error. For this sample, the economies of scale offset the additional costs to the approximate levels of the percentages found for the other samples.

Table 7. Administration Expenses, Additional Cost of Branch Banks Over Unit Banks

Number of Branches	Additional Cost Computed at Geometric Means			Percentage Increase in Cost		
	1959	1960	1961	1959	1960	1961
1	$2,670	$ 7,680	$2,440	4.0%	8.1%	3.5
2	4,300	12,480	3,780	6.4	13.2	5.4
3	5,460	16,210	4,980	8.1	17.2	7.1
4	6,300	19,410	5,670	9.4	20.2	8.1
8	—	25,210	7,430	—	26.8	10.7

Table 8. Administration Expenses, Additional Costs of Branch Banking (A) and Cost Savings Due to Scale of Operations, in Percentages

Number of Branches	Additional Cost of Branch Banking at New Scale of Operations $(A \times E)$			Cost Savings Due to Scale of Operations $(1 - E)$[a]			Net Addition to Costs $(A \times E) - (1 - E)$		
	1959	1960	1961	1959	1960	1961	1959	1960	1961
1	4.0	7.4	3.5	0.5	8.4	0.3	3.5	−1.0	3.2
2	6.4	12.1	5.4	0.5	8.4	0.3	5.9	3.7	5.1
3	8.1	15.8	7.1	0.5	8.4	0.3	7.6	7.4	6.8
4	9.4	18.5	8.1	0.5	8.4	0.3	8.9	10.2	7.8
8	—	24.5	10.7	—	8.4	0.3	—	16.2	10.4

[a] Economies of scale (and the standard errors of the coefficients) with respect to total assets are .995 (.051) for 1959, .916 (.052) for 1960, and .997 (.076) for 1961.

Business promotion expenses

Business promotion expenses are the smallest of the indirect expenses—only 5 per cent of total operating expenses. Approximately 68 per cent of the business promotion expenses went for advertising and publicity, 22 per cent for donations and gifts and the balance for travel. TA, B/LS and I/LS are significant at "explaining" these expenses. None of the forms of the branch banking variables were "significant," nor were economies or diseconomies of scale found.[28]

Occupancy expenses

Occupancy expenses are different from the other expenses discussed above because they obviously are a function of branch banking *per se*. Approximately 11 per cent of total operating expenses are occupancy expenses, which consist of building maintenance and depreciation less building rent received, if any. Depreciation, the most unreliable expense element included in the study, made up only 19 per cent of occupancy expenses.

Regressions were computed from the 1959 and 1960 samples, only, since a change in reporting in 1961 resulted in non-comparable data. The square of TA was superior to TA in "explaining" the dependent variable. In addition to this "scale" variable and the branch bank dummy variables, D/TD and I/LS are "significant."[29] The regression coefficients of the branch banking dummy variables are two to three times larger than their standard errors, except for the B^1 (one branch) variable. For this variable, the coefficients (and standard errors) are .039 (.041) for 1959 and .047 (.042) for 1960. Thus, the additional occupancy costs of a one branch bank presented in Table 9 are not very reliable.

Table 9. Occupancy Expenses, Additional Cost of Branch Banks Over Unit Banks

Number of Branches	Additional Cost Computed at Geometric Means		Percentage Increase in Cost	
	1959	1960	1959	1960
1 (B_1)	$ 2,230	$ 3,650	9.4	11.4
2 (B_2)	4,900	6,830	20.8	21.3
3 (B_3)	8,910	7,460	37.7	23.3
4 (B_4)	27,510	26,220	116.8	82.0
5+ (B_5)	—	12,580	—	39.3

The finding of large additional occupancy expenses for banks operating from more than one office (reported in Table 9) is not surpris-

[28] The coefficients (elasticities) of TA are .956 (.075), for 1959, .991 (.054) for 1960 and 1.055 (.087) for 1961 (standard errors are given in the parentheses).

[29] The population of the county in which each bank is located was tried as an independent variable, since occupancy expense may be a function of size of community. However, it was not significant, since the regression coefficient was less than half the size of its standard error. R^2's of the regressions are .86 for 1959 and .89 for 1960. Standard error of estimate percentages are 31 for 1959 and 31 for 1960.

ing, since it is expected that it is more expensive to conduct the same volume of operations from more than one office. In addition, the data presented do not represent the estimated extra expenses that would be incurred if several unit banks merged to form a single branch bank (as do the data given above for the other banking services and indirect administration expenses) since there is no reason to expect occupancy expenses to change. Rather, the data in Table 9 show the additional occupancy costs of a branch bank over a unit bank that holds the same average level of total assets. These additional costs, then, should not be considered as estimates of the cost of relatively less efficient branch operations.

Occupancy expenses were subject to negligible economies of scale that are not constant over the range of total assets sampled. At the geometric means of TA, the elasticities (E) (and their ranges from mean less one standard deviation to mean plus one standard deviation) are .915 (.882 to .949) in 1959 and .998 (.955 to 1.041) in 1960. Table 10 summarizes the joint effect on expenses of additional branch expenses and elasticities.

Table 10. Occupancy Expenses, Additional Costs of Branch Banking (A) and Cost Savings Due to Scale of Operations, in Percentages

Number of Branches	Additional Cost of Branch Banking at New Scale of Operations (A × E)		Cost Savings Due to Scale of Operations (1 − E)[a]		Net Addition to Costs (A × E) − (1 − E)	
	1959	1960	1959	1960	1959	1960
1 (B₁)	8.6	10.9	8.7	1.4	—0.1	9.5
2 (B₂)	19.0	21.4	6.4	−1.1	12.6	22.5
3 (B₃)	35.6	24.1	5.6	−3.6	30.0	27.7
4 (B₄)	110.3	84.3	4.7	−2.8	105.6	87.1
5+ (B₅)	—	41.9	—	−6.7	—	58.6

[a] Elasticities are computed at the average level of total assets held by each type of branch banking system.

IV. A Summary of the Findings

Higher costs for branch banking were found consistently among the samples for the demand deposits and the instalment loans services and for occupancy expenses. Higher costs were also found for indirect administration expenses and for the time deposits services, but the coefficients from which these are estimated had relatively large standard errors or were inconsistent in magnitude among the samples. Business loans, mortgage loans, securities and indirect business development expenses appear to be unaffected by the branch or unit form of organization.

Economies of scale were found for all of the banking services and indirect expenses except for business loans and indirect business promotion expenses. However, the elasticities measured were not much less than unity, in most cases.

The over-all effects on total bank operations costs of branch banking and economies of scale are summarized in Table 11. The percentages tabulated were determined by (1) computing for each sample, at the geometric means, the percentage of total operations expenses due to each banking service and type of indirect expense, and (2) multiplying the percentage by the net percentage increase or decrease in costs due to the joint effects of additional branch banking costs and economies of scale (as given in the tables presented above in Section III). The product is the net estimated percentage increase or decrease in operating costs caused by branch banking and economies of scale. These percentages are given for each of the samples so that the reader can judge the stability of the estimates.

Except for occupancy expenses, Table 11 shows the average net increase or decrease in the sum of their operating expenses that two or more unit banks would experience if they merged to form a branch bank (not including the temporary costs of merging and assuming, of course, that their experience would be that measured for the sampled banks). Thus, if five unit banks merged to form a branch bank with four branches, the total demand deposit operations expenses of the new branch are expected to be 4.7 per cent higher than the sum of these expenses of the five unit banks. However, this reasoning does not apply to occupancy expenses. Table 11 shows only that the occupancy expenses of the four branch bank, to continue the example, are 13.9 per cent higher than those of a unit bank that processes the same volume of output. The 13.9 per cent increase, then, is the additional cost of serving the same number of customers from five locations instead of one—it may be more or less than the sum of the occupancy costs of the five original unit banks.

The distinction just mentioned between occupancy expenses and the other groups of operations expenses is important when banking policy is considered. Given that banking is a regulated industry with restricted entry, it is necessary to determine whether the net increases in operations costs that branch banks experience are offset by the convenience benefits to the public of being served by more than one banking office.[30] The additional cost of occupancy is different from other additional operations

[30] If banking were a free market (with respect to entry and non-collusive practices among banks), the public would determine this question by their patronage.

expenses because it is the cost of providing additional convenience. Further, the average percentage increase in expenses due to occupancy expenses are 49 per cent of the total gross increase found for branch banks with four and over branches. The demand deposits service accounted for 26 per cent, instalment loans for 10 per cent, and administration expenses for 15 per cent of the total gross increase, on the average, for banks with four and more branches.

Table 11. Net Percentage Increase or Decrease in Operations Costs Due to the Joint Effect of Branch Banking and Economies of Scale

Banking Service or Type of Indirect Expense	Number of Branches				
	One	Two	Three	Four	Five and Over[a]
Demand deposits:					
1960	.0	1.4	.0	3.4	6.3
1961	.0	−2.1	.0	5.9	4.4
Average	.0	−0.4	.0	4.7	5.4
Instalment loans:					
1959	−0.4	0.5	1.1	1.6	—
1960	−0.5	0.1	0.6	1.0	2.0
1961	−0.5	0.4	1.1	1.6	3.1
Average	−0.5	0.3	0.9	1.4	2.6
Occupancy expenses:					
1959	.0	1.3	3.2	18.3	—
1960	1.0	2.4	3.0	9.4	6.4
Average	0.5	1.9	3.1	13.9	6.4
Sub-Total, percentages computed from "reliable" coefficients	.0	1.8	4.0	20.0	14.4
Administration expenses:					
1959	1.0	1.1	2.1	2.5	—
1960	−0.3	1.0	2.0	2.8	4.4
1961	0.7	1.2	1.6	1.8	2.4
Average	0.5	1.1	1.9	2.4	3.4
Time deposits:					
1959	−1.3	0.2	−0.5	−1.3	—
1960	−0.2	−0.2	0.8	−0.2	−0.2
1961	−0.6	−0.6	0.7	1.5	−0.6
Average	−0.7	−0.2	0.3	.0	−0.4

Table 11. Net Percentage Increase or Decrease in Operations Costs Due to the Joint Effect of Branch Banking and Economies of Scale (continued)

Banking Service or Type of Indirect Expense	Number of Branches				
	One	Two	Three	Four	Five and Over[a]
Mortgage loans:					
1959	−0.3	−0.3	−0.3	−0.3	—
1960	−0.3	−0.3	−0.3	−0.3	−0.3
1961	−0.4	−0.4	−0.4	−0.3	−0.3
Average	−0.3	−0.3	−0.3	−0.3	−0.3
Securities:					
1959	−0.3	−0.4	−0.4	−0.5	—
1960	−0.2	−0.5	−0.2	−0.6	−0.5
1961	−0.3	−0.3	−0.1	.0	−0.3
Average	−0.3	−0.4	−0.2	−0.4	−0.4
Total	−0.8	2.0	5.7	21.7	16.7

[a] Where the number of offices variable (NO) was used, the computation is for banks with eight branches. None of the banks in the 1959 sample had more than four branches.

Another important finding is that one and two branch banks have costs that are not much different than those of unit banks. This is an interesting finding, considering that researchers most often label banks as unit or branch, on the assumption that this dichotomy is useful. It appears better to group one and two branch banks with unit banks, at least for cost studies.

V. Comparison of the Findings with Those of Previous Studies

The conclusions drawn from this study, summarized above, are limited by the data used. The applicability of the findings may be assessed by comparing them with two other published studies made by Paul M. Horvitz[31] and Irving Schweiger and John S. McGee[32] that used data from all member banks.[33] This comparison indicates that the data used

[31] Paul M. Horvitz, "Economies of Scale in Banking," in *Private Financial Institutions*, the Commission on Money and Credit, Prentice-Hall (Englewood Cliffs, New Jersey: 1963), 1-54.

[32] Irving Schweiger and John S. McGee, "Chicago Banking," *Journal of Business*, XXXIV (1961), 203-366.

[33] David A. Alhadeff's *Monopoly and Competition in Banking, University of California Press* (Berkeley: 1954) is the first published empirical study of the comparative costs of branch and unit banks. However, his findings cannot be usefully

for my study are representative of all U.S. banks in the size range sampled. However, the findings of this study and the others differ because of the methods of analysis used and the detail of the data available.

Horvitz's study was made for the Commission on Money and Credit. He used data from all Federal Reserve member banks for 1959, separating this sample into three groups, depending on the ratio of time to total deposits they held. Horvitz found that:

> For any given size and time deposit ratio, the branch bank expenses were greater (with only one exception) than the unit bank costs. What is important is not only the fact that branch bank costs were higher but also the considerable spread between branch and unit bank costs. This spread was generally greater than the spread between banks of different sizes. This means, surprisingly enough, that four $15-million unit banks can be operated at a lower cost than a $60-million branch bank. In fact, even the smallest size category unit banks had lower costs, on average, than the largest size branch banks (except for banks with less than 25 per cent time deposits). The differences here are small but they indicate that extension of branch banking need not mean the demise of the small unit bank.[34]

Unfortunately, it is not clear that these findings indicate more than differences in product mix between branch and unit banks.[35] Horvitz's data show that the branch banks held greater proportions of instalment and mortgage loans to total loans and securities than unit banks. These are more expensive to process, per dollar loaned or invested, than are business loans and investments. Another important qualification is that measuring operating efficiency in terms of costs per dollars loaned and invested confuses economies due to large scale operations with those due to serving customers with large deposit balances or loans.

Schweiger and McGee used multiple regression analyses on operating ratio data from all member banks for 1959 to explain total operating costs per thousand dollars of asset ("unit" costs). "Unit" costs were regressed on size of bank in millions of dollars of deposits, branch-unit dummy variable, where branch $= 1$ and unit $= 0$, and six other independent variables which accounted for the ratios of business, consumer and farm loans to total asset, time deposits to total deposits, percentage growth of state population, and size of community.[36] They divided their

---

compared with those reported above because (as he points out in his book) unaccounted for differences between branch and unit banks in such particulars as the type of loans made, the size of loans and deposit structure, make it very difficult to interpret his results.

[34] *Ibid.*, 37-38.

[35] David A. Alhadeff similarly criticized these data limitations in his review of *Private Financial Institutions, Journal of Finance,* XIX (September, 1964), 521.

[36] The following R^2's are reported: under $50 million in deposits group, .25; $50 to $200 million in deposits group, .43; and over $200 million group, .67. Standard errors of estimate are not given.

sample into three groups and found substantial "economics of scale" only for banks holding less than $50 million in deposits. Additional branch banking costs of $235 per thousand dollars of asset also were estimated. For these banks, they conclude that "a branch bank with $17 million greater deposits than a unit bank should, other things being the same, have an equal or lower expense rate."[37] However, they found no commensurate offsetting savings for larger branch banks, although additional branch banking costs averaging $338 per thousand dollars of assets were found.[38]

To compare my study with that of Schweiger and McGee, the regression on the 1959 sample (the data year of their study) was recomputed, using the same dependent variable and most of the same independent variables. The regression coefficients for their sample of banks with less than $50 million in deposits have the same signs and almost the same magnitudes as those similarly computed from the data used in my study. In addition, the percentage increase in branch bank costs over unit bank costs found by Horvitz and by Schweiger and McGee are quite close to those given in Table 11. It is evident, then, that my study at least is consistent with the findings of the other studies and the samples used representative of all member banks in this size range.

Nevertheless, our findings are not the same. The other studies found substantial "economies" of large scale operation. However, I believe that this discrepancy may be due to the fact that larger banks tend to serve customers with larger deposit accounts or loans. By using costs per dollar of assets ("unit" costs) one is in danger of making the not surprising or useful conclusion that a wholesale operation is more "efficient" than a retail operation. The relevant question is whether larger banks service the *same type* of customers at lower or higher cost than smaller banks. With output defined as the number of deposit accounts and loans and other factors that affect operating costs accounted for, I found but slight economies of scale.

All of the studies revealed higher costs of branch banks *per se*, over unit banks. In my more detailed analysis, approximately half of these costs were found to be due to occupancy expenses. The balance of the higher costs amounted to 7.8 per cent of operating costs for banks with four branches, 10.3 per cent for banks with five or more branches, and negligible amounts for banks with less than four branches. Thus, it appears that the higher branch banking costs found by previous researchers

[37] *Ibid.*, p. 326.

[38] Lyle E. Gramley also used multiple regression analysis with similar variables for a study of Tenth Federal Reserve District Banks except that his sample included only unit banks. (*A Study of Scale Economies in Banking*, Federal Reserve Bank of Kansas City, Kansas City: 1962.) His findings with respect to "unit" costs and bank size as measured by total assets were consistent with those reported by Schweiger and McGee.

could be due in large measure to additional occupancy expenses, rather than to inefficiencies in operation or administration.

VI. Conclusions

Because the population from which the samples were drawn is limited to medium sized banks, one hesitates to draw conclusions that may be applied to the entire banking system. With this understanding, the following conclusions are offered.

The study shows that branch banking does entail additional costs that are not offset by economies of scale. Analysis of these costs reveals that (1) branch banks with one and two branches do not have costs that are very different from those of unit banks, (2) approximately half of the additional costs are due to occupancy expenses, and (3) the marginal cost of additional branches beyond eight probably is very small. The additional occupancy expenses may be excluded as "extra" costs for policy considerations, because there is no evidence that the total costs expended on occpancy by, say, five unit banks would be greater than those expended by one branch bank with four branches, assuming that it processed the same volume of output as the unit banks. With additional occupancy expenses omitted, the costs of branch banks with three branches do not appear to be very different from those of similar sized unit banks and branch banks with four and over branches experience additional costs that average approximately 9 per cent of total operating expenses.

It does not necessarily follow from these findings that charges would be higher to depositors and borrowers of branch banks. Other differences between branch and unit banks, such as ability and desire to take risks, may offset or reinforce differences in operating expenses.

Thus, the conclusions that can be reached must be limited to a statement of the fact that, exclusive of occupancy costs, additional operating expenses for the banks sampled average approximately 9 per cent. Whether these costs are offset by the convenience to the public of having more offices at which to bank, or by other factors, or whether the magnitude of the costs are different for larger banks than those sampled, remain questions for policy makers and future research.

5

Commercial bank price discrimination
against small loans: An empirical study*

George J. Benston†

The business loan surveys made by the Federal Reserve Board[1]
reveal consistently that commercial bank loans of smaller sizes carry
higher interest rates than do larger loans. Since size of loans and size of
firm are highly correlated, this inverse relationship between interest rates
and size of loans apparently has led many observers to conclude that
banks discriminate against small businesses.[2] It is reasoned that small
businesses have fewer sources of funds available to them and hence have
more inelastic demand curves for loans from a particular bank lender
than have large businesses. The banks are thought to "take advantage" of
this situation by charging higher interest rates on small loans than on
large loans.

An alternative hypothesis is that the observed differential between
interest rates charged on large and small loans is due to a differential
in the marginal costs of lending and risk between large and small loans.
The elasticity of demand for loans faced by a bank is believed to be the

Reprinted with permission from *The Journal of Finance*, Vol. XIX, No. 4 (December, 1964), pp. 631-643.

* The research upon which this paper is based was supported by the Federal
Reserve Bank of Chicago and the Ford Foundation, to whom grateful acknowledge-
ment is made. Messrs. John Hayes and Richard Matulis of the Federal Reserve Bank
of Boston provided valuable support in the gathering of the basic data. Of course they
bear no responsibility for the way the data were used or the conclusions drawn from
them.

† Assistant Professor, The University of Chicago Graduate School of Business.
[1] Conducted in 1942, 1946, 1955, and 1957 and published in [1], [4], [5], and
[15]. [*Editors' note*: Reference numbers are for the list at the end of this article.]
[2] A.M. Levenson cites many sources in [10], and [11, footnote 2, p. 190].

same whether it is derived from large or small loans.[3] Then, as one can demonstrate with familiar price theory analysis, higher marginal costs of lending and risk on small loans (if they exist) should be reflected in higher rates charged on these loans if the bank does not price discriminate against large loans.[4]

To demonstrate this alternative hypothesis, it is necessary not only to show that the marginal cost of lending and risk is higher for small than for large loans, but also to show that the difference in marginal costs is sufficient to explain the difference in marginal earnings.[5] Thus, estimates of marginal earnings, marginal lending costs, and the marginal cost of risk per $100 change in the size of loans, with the effect of other relevant factors taken into account, are presented in this study. Data for 1959 and 1960 and 1961 (three cross sections) were analyzed by means of multiple regression analysis. The coefficients estimated were consistent among the cross sections. Marginal costs were found to increase as the size of loans decreased, *cet. par.* These higher marginal costs of smaller loans accounted for approximately 76 per cent of the differential in marginal earnings between larger and smaller loans. The remaining differential, although in the direction of discrimination against small loans, is so small that it cannot be given much importance and may be attributable to lower interest rates given to large borrowers in lieu of interest payments on their demand deposits, or to sampling error.

In addition, these data provide a test of the hypothesis that banks discriminate more against small borrowers than against large borrowers in periods of tighter money. If this hypothesis obtained, we would find that the banks made relatively greater marginal earnings from small loans than from large loans in tighter money periods than in easier periods. In fact, the data do not show this and thus are inconsistent with the hypothesis.

The data on which these conclusions are based and the statistical techniques used to analyze them are discussed in the following two sections. The findings of the analysis are presented in detail in Sections III, IV and V and summarized in Section VI. In particular, estimates are given of marginal earnings, marginal lending cost, and the marginal cost of risk per $100 change in the average size of business loans. A test of the hypothesis about greater bank discrimination against small borrowers in relatively tighter money periods is presented in Section VII.

---

[3] For example, see [12] and [13].

[4] This hypothesis was most recently discussed by Levenson [11].

[5] The data that Levenson [11] had at his disposal did not allow him to compute marginal lending costs and earnings nor the cost of risk. He found that the average cost per dollar of loans was lower for large loans than small loans, though the large errors of his estimates were such as to make his findings suggestive rather than conclusive.

I. The Data

The basic data were gathered by the Federal Reserve Bank of Boston as a by-product of a cost accounting and analysis service for medium-sized First District member banks. This service has been provided since 1957 and is limited to banks with total assets of between $3.5 and $55.0 million.[6] The Bank held seminars on cost analysis, provided instruction booklets, advice, and forms, and checked and tabulated the data for those banks that wished to participate. The participating banks allocated earnings and direct costs to the banking services of demand deposits, time deposits, installment loans, mortgage loans, business loans, and investments, and listed indirect costs separately. These data were used to prepare reports for each bank in which its costs for each banking service were compared with those of banks with services of similar size.

These basic data (and data on charged-off loans gathered for this paper) were used to compute the annual marginal earnings and costs reported below. These estimates were made for each of three cross sections. The cross sections include 83 banks for 1959, 82 banks for 1960, and 80 banks for 1961.[7] Thus, the study was replicated twice.

II. Variables Used in the Statistical Analysis

A test of the hypothesis that differences in interest rates charged on large and small loans can be accounted for by differences in cost requires estimates of (1) the marginal earnings from lending due to size of loans, (2) the marginal cost of lending due to size of loans and (3) the marginal cost of risk due to size of loans.[8] Multiple regression analysis was used to take into account the effect of factors other than the size of loans on marginal earnings and costs. Total earnings, lending cost, and risk cost were regressed on size of loans and other relevant factors, and the resulting equations were differentiated with respect to size of loans to compute marginal earnings and costs. The variables used for the regressions are discussed in this section of the paper and the estimated coefficients and computed marginal earnings and costs are given in the following section.

The dependent variables used for the analyses were:

---

[6] The upper limit was lower for the years before 1959.

[7] Of these, 50 banks are included in all three cross sections.

[8] Hereafter, "loans" when used without qualification refers to business loans only.

1. E   = Annual earnings from loans
2. DC = Annual direct lending cost
3. CO = The mean of total business, installment and mortgage loans
          charged-off in a year and the amount charged-off in the fol-
          lowing year.

Annual earnings from loans (E) include interest and service charges. Had service charges not been included, the estimates computed might have biased the study in favor of the hypothesis that interest differentials can be explained by cost differentials. It is reasonable to assume that banks would compensate for some higher costs of lending or risk on small loans by increasing service charges in addition to charging higher interest rates. Including service charges with interest earned thus avoids a possible downward bias on the interest rates of smaller loans. The possible effect of minimum balance requirements was not taken into account, which may have resulted in an understatement of the interest rates earned on large loans and thus bias the findings of this study against the "cost" hypothesis. However, the role of compensating balances is not clear, and there is reason to doubt that they do affect actual interest rates charged.[9]

Annual direct lending costs (DC) were allocated to the business loan service as described above. The cost of acquiring loanable funds, a major portion of the cost of business loans, was not considered, since there is no reason to expect a cost difference per dollar loaned for large or small loans.[10] In addition, inclusion of the cost of funds probably would have resulted in biasing the findings toward lower marginal costs on large loans. Economies of scale in deposit services [3, pp. 40-1] and the positive correlation of bank size and size of loans [9] would have produced this bias. Similarly, indirect lending costs were not considered.[11]

The mean of two years' annual charged-off business, installment and mortgage loans (C) was used as the dependent variable to estimate the cost of risk due to differences in loan size. Charged-off business loans

---

[9] To do so, a borrower would have to hold a greater deposit balance than he would have had he not borrowed. Rather, compensating balance requirements have the effect of guaranteeing that the borrower maintains his balances with the bank. This requirement is necessary if the bank gave the borrower-depositor lower rates on his loan in lieu of the direct payment of interest on his deposit, since the latter is illegal. (See [6] and [7].)

[10] One possible source of difference may result from an interrelationship of demand for loans and deposit services. To test for this possibility, the average yield on business loans was included as an independent variable in the 1960 cross section demand deposit service regression. This variable had a partial correlation coefficient of but .14 which, with 80 observations and eight independent variables, was not significant at the 5 per cent level. (See [3].)

[11] The (remote, I believe) possibility of a difference in indirect costs between large and small loans could not be tested statistically because of collinearity between the average size of demand deposit regular checking accounts and the average size of business loans.

only were not available. However, the average outstanding balances of installment and mortgage loans were included in the analyses as independent variables to take their effects into account. The mean of two successive years' charged-off loans was used, because actual losses on loans made in one year may not be charged-off until the following year.[12]

The independent variables used in the analyses include:

4. N = The number of loans outstanding
5. S = The average size of loans outstanding
6. Y = The yield earned per $1000 of loans
7. I = Average installment loans
8. M = Average mortgage loans
9. RL = The ratio of business loans to total loans and investment, in percentages
10. W = Wages per employee for the first quarter, 1959, of employees in banking and related industries in the county in which bank is located, and
11. B = The number of branches the bank operates.

The number of loans outstanding was measured at each month-end during the year. The variable used for the analysis, N, is the arithmetic mean of this series. The average size of loans, S, was computed by dividing the average total dollar amount of loans outstanding during the year by N. The denominator, average total loans outstanding, is the arithmetic mean of the total dollar amount of loans outstanding at each month-end during the year. These averaging procedures aid in reducing the effects of random fluctuations.

It should be noted that the independent variable of interest, the average size of loans (S), is an average of all loans (large and small) outstanding at a particular bank. The regression coefficients computed provide estimates of long run marginal costs and earnings. The marginal costs and earnings computed are estimates of the amounts a bank would incur or earn if it was able to increase the average size of its loans and adjust its operations to the new situation. Thus, differences in earnings and costs among banks rather than differences within a bank are estimated.[13]

The interest yield earned on business loans, Y, is the ratio of total loan income (interest and service charges) for the year, divided by

[12] The amount of loans charged-off in 1960 and 1961 were obtained for banks in the 1959 and 1960 studies that were not included in later cross sections. However, 1962 charge-offs could not be secured.

[13] Differences within a bank due to differences in loan size could be estimated from time series data to provide measures of short run marginal earnings and costs if the effects of other relevant variables could be taken into account and collinearity problems overcome. However, I believe that long run estimates are more useful than short run estimates because price and output decisions of banks are based on long run relationships with borrowers and depositors.

average total loans outstanding. Average installment and mortgage loans (I and M) are the mean of the balances outstanding at each month-end during a year.

The ratio of business loans to total loans and investments, RL, was computed by dividing the total average dollar amount of business loans outstanding by the mean of the total amount of loans and investments outstanding at each month-end during the year. This variable was included in the analysis to assess the magnitude of economies of scale in the short run due to the total size of a bank. Total assets were used first, but collinearity among this variable, the number of loans (N), and the average size of loans (S) dictated its replacement by RL. However, RL is a good substitute for total assets, since the logarithms of N and S are included with RL in the regression equations, and taking their joint effect into account is equivalent to taking account of the effect of total business loans (the denominator). The sign of the coefficient of RL, then, is due to fluctuations of total loans and investments, the numerator of the ratio.

The measure of relative wages, W, was included to account for differences in factor prices among geographical areas, since most of the direct expenses of lending are salary costs. The wage index was computed by dividing the number of employees in banking and similar industries (insurance, savings and loan associations, savings banks, and credit unions) as of March 15, 1959 into the total wages paid for the first quarter of 1959 by these industries in the county in which each bank is located. The relative wages variable, W, then, is the average wages paid for the first quarter per employee. The data for these computations were derived from social security (FICA) reports[14]. Since all wages paid up to $16,800 a year are reported in full on the first quarter FICA returns, and since all banks are required to file the return, the index is not likely to be biased by exclusion of data.

The final factor listed, the number of branches operated by a bank, was included to account for cost differences due to the form of a bank's organization. Several forms of this variable were used, but all were found to be of little or no significance. (The standard errors of the regression coefficients estimated were several times the size of the coefficients.) Hence, the branches variable was excluded from the analysis.

Variables (1) through (10), then, were used in a multiple regression analysis. All variables were transformed to common logarithms for two reasons. First, the multiplicative form of the marginal cost function was believed to reflect most accurately the relationships among the variables. Thus, the level of the marginal cost of a unit change in the average size of loans is a function of the magnitude of the other variables included in the regression. Second, use of the logarithmic form resulted in the achievement of approximate homoscedasticity, while the untransformed variables were found to be heteroscedastic.

The squares of the logarithms of N and S were included in the regressions, since these forms, together with the linear logarithms, enable one to approximate almost any theoretically recognized cost curve. However, their inclusion served only to increase the corrected standard error of estimate of the regressions and increase the standard errors of the regression coefficients of the linear forms. Hence, it was concluded that the cost functions were linear in logarithms.

III. Marginal Earnings

The logarithm of annual earnings from loans (E) was regressed on the logarithms of the average size of loans (S) and the number of loans (N) for each cross section. The logarithm of the ratio (in percentages) of business loans to total loans and investments (RL) was included at first, but it was found to be insignificant.[14] The relative wages variable (W) was not used because it relates to costs, not earnings. The equation used to analyze each cross section, then, was:

1. $$\log_{10}E = \log_{10}a + b\log_{10}S + c\log_{10}N,$$

where a is the sample constant term, and b and c are sample regression coefficients. The constant term and coefficients estimated are given in the table below. (Standard errors appear in parentheses beneath the coefficients.)

Table 1. Regressions of Log_{10} Annual Earnings, Coefficients and Standard Errors

Independent Variables $(\log_{10})$	Cross Section		
	1959	1960	1961
S (average size of loans)	.951	.950	.947
	(.017)	(.023)	(.016)
N (number of loans)	1.016	1.012	1.000
	(.018)	(.024)	(.016)
Constant term	1.843	−1.126	−1.085
Standard error of estimate	.0421	.0612	.0410
R^2 (footnote 15)	.9970	.9990	.9976
Number of observations	83	82	80

[14] The rule used in this study for exclusion of a variable because of "insignificance" was that the standard error of its regression coefficient be larger than the coefficient.

[15] The high R^2's are to be expected, since the product of N and S equals total loans outstanding, a variable which, we would expect, determines total earnings. However, we are interested in the regression coefficient of S, rather than with the determinants of earnings.

Marginal earnings per $100 change in the average size of a loan (ME) were computed at the geometric mean of N. Thus, ME was derived from the first derivative of equation (1), as follows:

2.
$$ME = \frac{100}{\bar{\bar{N}}} (aS^{b-1}\bar{\bar{N}}^c)$$

where N denotes the geometric mean of N. Marginal earnings were computed for several values of S. These computations are given in Table 4 below together with estimates of marginal costs. The slopes of marginal earnings are negative and approximately equal for all three cross sections. However, the level of marginal earnings in 1959 is higher than the levels for 1960 and 1961.

IV. Marginal Lending Cost

The logarithm of annual direct lending cost (DC) was regressed on the logarithms of the average size of loans (S), the number of loans (N), the yield earned on loans (Y), the ratio of business loans to total loans and investments, in percentages (RL), and relative wages (W). Thus, the equation used to analyze each cross section was:

3.
$$\log_{10}DC = \log_{10}f + g\log_{10}S + h\log_{10}N + i\log_{10}Y + j\log_{10}RL + k\log_{10}W,$$

where f is the sample constant term, and g, h, i, j and k are sample regression coefficients. The constant term and coefficients estimated are given in Table 2 below. (Standard errors appear in parentheses beneath the coefficients.)

From these regressions, the annual marginal direct cost of lending an additional $100 of business loans was computed. In making these computations, all the variables except $\log_{10}S$ and $\log_{10}Y$ were held constant at their geometric mean values. $\log_{10}Y$ was allowed to vary in order to test hypotheses about the relationship of marginal yields and marginal costs due to differences in size of loans. The sign of coefficients computed above for Y indicate that banks with higher average loan sizes incurred higher lending costs. They also earned higher marginal income. Thus, the effect on lending cost of the variation of $\log_{10}Y$ and $\log_{10}S$ must be taken into account. The other variables, though, may be held constant at their geometric means. Equation (3) must be written, then, in antilogarithms, as:

4.
$$DC = fS^g\bar{\bar{N}}^hY^i\overline{RL}^j\bar{\bar{W}}^k,$$

Table 2. Regressions of Log_{10} Direct Cost, Coefficients and Standard Errors

Independent Variables (log_{10})	Cross Section		
	1959	1960	1961
S (average size of loans)	.740	.810	.851
	(.086)	(.073)	(.096)
N (number of loans)	.978	.919	1.006
	(.081)	(.066)	(.084)
Y (yield on loans)	1.708	.915	.993
	(.436)	(.340)	(.513)
W (relative wages)	1.007	.560	.540
	(.338)	(.288)	(.366)
RL (ratio of business loans to total loans and investments, in percentages)	−.246	−.301	−.250
	(.117)	(.112)	(.157)
Constant term	−6.263	−4.489	−3.618
Standard error of estimate	.1600	.1537	.1811
R^2	.7906	.8263	.7921
Number of observations	83	82	80

where bars denote geometric means. The annual marginal direct cost of lending per \$100 change in average size of loans (MCL) is the first derivative of equation (4), with Y allowed to vary with S, and N, RL, and W held constant at their geometric mean values, as follows:

5. $$MCL = \frac{100}{\overline{N}}\left[gfS^{g-1}\overline{N}^h Y^i \overline{RL}^j \overline{W}^k + \frac{\sigma Y}{\sigma S}\left(ifS^g \overline{N}^h Y^{i-1}\overline{RL}^j \overline{W}^k \right) \right]$$

To compute MCL, logY had to be regressed on logS.[16] Equation (5) was evaluated at various levels of S, at the levels of Y determined by the levels of S chosen (computed from the regression equations given in footnote 16) and at the geometric means of the other variables for the coefficients estimated. The results of these computations are presented in Table 4 below.

These estimates of the annual marginal direct cost of lending due to a \$100 change in the average size of loans were found to have negative

[16] The regression coefficients (and standard errors) were as follows:
1959: Y = .913 − .053S
              (.016)
1960: Y = 1.912 − .051S
              (.024)
1961: Y = 1.899 − .052S
              (.0160)

slopes of similar magnitudes for all three cross sections. Thus, marginal lending cost is a function of the average size of loans. However, differences in marginal lending costs were sufficient to explain only about half of the differences in marginal earnings due to average loan size differences.

V. Marginal Cost of Risk

Risk (CO) was measured by the mean of the total dollar amount of all loans charged off in a year and in the following year at a particular bank. The following regressions were computed for the 1959 and 1960 cross sections:

6. $$\log_{10}CO = \log_{10}m + n\log_{10}S + p\log_{10}N, + q\log_{10}I$$

where m is the sample constant term, and n, p, and q are sample regression coefficients. Since 1962 charge-offs could not be obtained, charge-offs in 1961 only were used as the dependent variable for the 1961 cross section.[17] The coefficients and standard errors computed are given in Table 3 below.[18]

The marginal annual cost of risk (MCR) was computed by differentiating equation 6 and using the coefficients estimated above. Thus, the marginal annual cost of risk per \$100 change in the average size of loans (MCR) was computed from equation (7):

7. $$\text{MCR} = \frac{100}{\overline{N}}(nmS^{n-1}\overline{N}^p\overline{I}^q)$$

where $\overline{N}$ and $\overline{I}$ are the geometric means of N and I. MCR, estimated at several values of S for each cross section, is given in Table 4. For all three cross sections, MCR declines as the average size of loans increases. The slope and magnitude of the curve is almost the same for 1960 and 1961 cross sections, but somewhat steeper and higher for the 1959 cross section.

---

[17] Average mortgage loans were included initially in the regressions, since the dependent variable may include charge-offs of mortgage loans. However, inclusion of this variable increased the corrected standard error of estimate and its regression coefficients were negative and smaller than the standard errors of the coefficients for all three cross sections. The regression coefficients of the other variables virtually were unchanged as a result of the exclusion of average mortgage loans and the computed marginal cost of risk was almost the same with average mortgage loans in or out of the equations.

[18] Regressions were also computed with $\log_{10}$ charged-off loans in the cross section year only as the dependent variable. The regression coefficients (and standard errors) estimated for S were .483 (.218) in 1959 and .725 (.309) in 1960. The R^2's for the two regressions were .1904 and .3252.

Table 3. Regressions of $\log_{10}$ Mean Charged-Off Loans, Coefficients and Standard Errors

Independent Variables ($\log_{10}$)	Cross Section		
	1959	1960	1961
S (average size of loans)	.558	.643	.459
	(.181)	(.256)	(.345)
N (number of loans)	.952	1.502	.822
	(.189)	(.249)	(.358)
I (average installment loans)	.120	.065	.519
	(.064)	(.093)	(.282)
Constant term	−1.425	−3.107	−3.368
Standard error of estimate	.4348	.6299	.7226
R^2	.3356	.3702	.2697
Number of observations	83	82	80

VI. Net Marginal Earnings—Summary and Conclusions

Table 4 summarizes the marginal earnings and costs computed from the coefficients estimated by the multiple regression analyses. Marginal lending cost and the marginal cost of risk were subtracted from gross marginal earnings to arrive at net marginal earnings. This is the estimated change in net profit (before the cost of funds, indirect expenses and income taxes) the banks earned per $100 change in the average size of loan, with the effect of other factors taken into account.

Marginal earnings from large and small loans (defined here as the geometric mean of the average size of loans plus and minus two standard deviations) were of the following percentage relationships prior to and after deducting marginal costs. (See Table 5.) Thus, by taking account of the marginal costs of lending and risk, 76 per cent (on average) of the estimated difference in marginal earnings between large and small loans could be explained.

The remaining difference may be due to concessions on lending rates given to larger borrowers in lieu of interest payments on their demand deposit accounts,[19] since average size of loans and average size of demand deposit accounts at the banks were positively correlated.[20] The marginal cost per dollar of processing a large account is much less than the marginal cost per dollar of processing a small account [3, pp.

[19] Cf., footnote 9 above and [8].
[20] Sample correlation coefficients of $\log_{10}$ average size of demand deposit accounts (excluding special checking accounts) were .575 for the 1960 cross section and .660 for the 1961 cross section. (Data were not available for 1959.)

Table 4. Annual Marginal Earnings, Marginal Lending Cost and
Marginal Risk per $100 Change in Average Business Loan Size

	At Values of Average Loan Size[a]				
Year of Cross Section	Mean Less Two St. Dev.	Mean Less One St. Dev.	Geometric Mean	Mean Plus One St. Dev.	Mean Plus Two St. Dev.
1959					
Gross marginal earnings	$7.504	$7.286	$7.061	$6.844	$6.609
Marginal lending cost[b]	.679	.545	.435	.348	.277
Marginal cost of risk	.393	.296	.222	.168	.126
Total marginal cost	1.072	.841	.657	.516	.403
Net marginal earnings	$6.432	$6.445	$6.404	$6.328	$6.206
Average loan size	$ 904	$ 1720	$ 3273	$ 6226	$11,840
1960					
Gross marginal earnings	$5.587	$5.384	$5.211	$5.043	$4.993
Marginal lending cost[b]	.694	.599	.519	.450	.389
Marginal cost of risk	.294	.231	.183	.145	.113
Total marginal cost	.988	.830	.702	.595	.502
Net marginal earnings	$4.599	$4.554	$4.509	$4.448	$4.491
Average loan size	$ 997	$ 1962	$ 3773	$ 7254	$14,270
1961					
Gross marginal earnings	$5.361	$5.177	$4.999	$4.826	$4.660
Marginal lending cost[b]	.790	.692	.608	.532	.466
Marginal cost of risk	.254	.177	.125	.087	.061
Total marginal cost	1.044	.869	.733	.619	.527
Net marginal earnings	$4.317	$4.308	$4.266	$4.205	$4.133
Average loan size	$ 1054	$ 2034	$ 3926	$ 7575	$14,620

[a] These values were chosen simply to provide the reader with a range of values along the curves.

[b] The secular increase in marginal lending costs indicated by the data may be due to increases in factor costs. Unfortunately, the available data do not allow a test of this belief.

25-45]. Thus, marginal earnings are greater on large accounts than on small accounts, *cet. par.*, and banks may compete for the balances of larger customers by giving them lower interest rates on their loans. Therefore the marginal gross and net earnings from larger loans may

Table 5. Percentage Relationships of Marginal Earnings Between Small and Large Loans Before and After Deducting Marginal Costs[a]

	1959	1960	1961
Gross marginal earnings: Large loans divided by small loans	1.135	1.119	1.150
Net marginal earnings: Large loans divided by small loans	1.036	1.024	1.044
Percentage difference on gross marginal earnings between large and small loans explained by deducting marginal costs	.747	.818	.738

[a] Computed from Table 4.

be understated, perhaps sufficiently to "explain" the remaining difference between the bank's marginal net earnings on large and small loans. Alternatively, the remaining difference may be taken as evidence that some price discrimination against small loans does exist. Or, the remaining differential in the net marginal earnings from small loans or large loans of 2 to 4 per cent (as shown in Table 5 above) simply may be due to estimation errors.

VII. Relative Discrimination in Tighter and Easier Money Periods

These data also bear on the hypothesis that banks tend to discriminate more against small borrowers in times of relative "tight" money and thus ration credit to them.[21] Three years of data are examined in the present study, of which one (1959) was a tighter money year and two (1960 and 1961) easier money years, as determined by the relative magnitudes of the gross marginal earnings realized by the sampled banks ($7.061 in 1959 and $5.211 and $4.999 in 1960 and 1961 per $100 at the geometric means of average loan size). Thus we can determine whether the differences in marginal earnings between years predicted by this hypothesis did, in fact, occur.

[21] Many other credit rationing hypotheses have been proposed and tested, notably the presumed refusal of banks to make, renew or reduce loans to small borrowers in tight money periods [2]. This hypothesis cannot be tested with the present data since relative demand conditions are not known. However, it is interesting to note that average loan sizes were not lower in the tighter money year (1959) than in the easier money years (1960 and 1961). Thus, if the demand in 1959 for smaller loans was not greater relative to the demand for larger loans, the data are inconsistent with this credit rationing hypothesis.

It is postulated that banks ration credit to smaller borrowers in tighter money periods by raising interest rates more to non-preferred (i.e., small) borrowers than to preferred (i.e., large) borrowers.[22] If this method of credit rationing were used, we would expect gross (and net) marginal earnings to be proportionately higher on small loans than large loans in the tighter money years than in the easier money years. However, the ratios presented in Table 5 above indicate that the predicted difference between years did not, in fact, occur. Hence, the data are inconsistent with the hypothesis.

VIII. Conclusions

Analysis of data from three cross sections of banks has revealed that differences in the marginal rate of interest charged by commercial banks on large and small loans can be explained largely by differences in the marginal cost of lending and in the marginal cost of risk. Further, the data are inconsistent with the hypothesis that banks discriminate against small borrowers in times of tight money.

Of course, it should be noted that the data on which these conclusions are based are far from perfect; the banks sampled are medium sized and hence reflect but a portion of the world of banking. And, the major output variable used for this study, the average size of business loans, is an aggregate measure of loan size at each bank sampled, and hence may mask differences within banks. However, the variables that are relevant for studying bank lending behavior—marginal earnings, marginal lending cost, and the marginal cost of risk—were estimated. These estimates were made for three cross sections and they were found to be consistent among the samples and statistically reliable. To this extent, our knowledge about banking operations is extended.

REFERENCES

1. G. L. Bach. "Interest Rates at Member Banks," *Fed. Res. Bull.*, Nov. 1942, 28, pp. 1089-1097.
2. G. L. Bach and C. J. Huizenga. "The Differential Effects of Tight Money," *Am. Econ. Rev.*, March. 1961, 51, pp. 52-80.
3. G. J. Benston, *The Cost of Banking Operation: A Statistical Study*, unpublished Ph.D. dissertation, The University of Chicago, 1963. See abstract in *Jour. Finance*, Mar. 1964, 19, pp. 111-12.

[22] Most recently, this argument was made by Laudadio [9].

4. J. B. Eckert. "Business Loans of Member Banks," *Fed. Res. Bull.*, April 1956, 42, pp. 327-40.
5. ———. "Member Bank Lending to Small Business, 1955-57," *Fed. Res. Bull.*, April 1958, 44, pp. 393-411.
6. R. E. Emmer. "Compensating Balances and the Cost of Loanable Funds," *Jour. Bus.*, October 1957, 30, pp. 261-75.
7. J. Guttentag and R. Davis. "Are Compensating Balance Requirements Irrational?" *Jour. Finance*, March 1962, 17, pp. 121-27.
8. D. R. Hodgman. "The Deposit Relationship and Commercial Bank Investment Behavior," *Rev. Econ. Stat.*, August 1961, 43, pp. 257-268.
9. L. Laudadio. "Size of Bank, Size of Borrower, and the Rate of Interest," *Jour. Finance*, March 1963, 18, pp. 20-28.
10. A. M. Levenson. *Differentials in Interest Rates and the Cost of Commercial Bank Lending*, unpublished Ph.D. dissertation, Columbia University, 1959.
11. ———. "Interest Rates and Cost Differentials in Bank Lending to Small and Large Business," *Rev. Econ. Stat.*, May 1962.
12. G. R. Miller, G. W. McKinley, and A. Choate. "Long-Term Small Business Financing," *Jour. Finance*, May 1961, 16, pp. 280-308.
13. I. Schweiger. "Adequacy of Financing for Small Business Since WW II," *Jour. Finance*, September 1958, 13, pp. 323-47.
14. U.S. Department of Commerce, U.S. Department of Health, Education and Welfare. *County Business Patterns*, First Quarter 1959, part 2, New England States, Washington: 1961.
15. R. Youngdahl. "The Structure of Interest Rates on Business Loans at Member Banks," *Fed. Res. Bull*, July 1947, 33, pp. 803-19.